1001 Internet Jokes Gay And Lesbian Edition

Get The Jokes You've Been Missing

D.M. Schwab
OPEN MIC PRESS
Toronto Vancouver New York London

INTRODUCTION

Here we are 10 years later and I'm still getting emailed jokes. For years, I've been sending and receiving some of the funniest emails in the English language. However, the internet has been a tool for other pranks, too. So, I'm also here to state some "Email Facts of Life" for you. First of all, Big companies don't do business via chain letter. Bill Gates is not giving you $1000, and Disney is not giving you a free vacation. There is no baby food company issuing class-action checks. You can relax; there is no need to pass it on "just in case it's true." Furthermore, just because someone said in the message, four generations back, that "we checked it out and it's legit," does not actually make it true. There is no kidney theft ring in New Orleans. No one's nephew's brother-in-law is waking up in a bathtub full of ice, even if a friend of a friend swears it happened to their nephew's brother-in-law. And I quote: "The National Kidney Foundation" has repeatedly issued requests for actual victims of organ thieves to come forward & tell their stories. None have. That's "none," as in "ZERO". Not even your friend's cousin. Oops, I guess I should confess that I don't think there are 1,001 Jokes in this book either.

However, by the bombardment of emails I both send and get it sure feels like there are. If you're CC: list is regularly longer than the actual content of your message, you're probably going to be punished eternally. (Ever heard of BCC:?) Instead of forwarding these jokes I've either edited or created, I have the decency to trim the eight miles of headers showing everyone else who's received it over the last 6 months and put it into a book for you to enjoy at your leisure.So relax and enjoy this truly humorous book.
Sincerely, D.M. Schwab
P.S. Another rumor I want to put to bed, Oprah is not gay.

ACKNOWLEDGEMENT

I would like to thank The Entire Greene Family, T. Tewsley, B.Nijjar, P. Saros, B. Besler, N. McIlroy, Kent B. Van Cleave, Dan Mohan, Will Dickinson, R. Windismann and all those who anonymously contributed jokes to the internet for their submissions and support throughout the years.

CHAPTER 1. - NUNS, PRIESTS AND OTHERS

An Anglo-Saxon missionary is sent to the deepest darkest jungle in Africa, to live with a tribe. He spends years with the tribe, teaching them to read, write, and the good Christian ways of the white man. One thing that he particularly stresses is the evils of sexual pleasure: "Must not commit adultery or fornication!" One day, the wife of one of the tribe's noblemen gave birth to a white child. The village is shocked, and the chief is then sent by his people to talk with the missionary. "You have taught us of the evils of sexual pleasure, yet here a black women gives birth to a white child. You are the only white man that has ever set foot in our village. I know what you've done!" The missionary tries to cover himself up by saying: "Oh, no, my good man—you are mistaken. What you have here is a natural occurrence, called an albino. LOOK TO THY YONDER FIELD! You see a field of white sheep, yet amongst them is one black sheep. Nature does this on occasion." The chief pauses a moment, and then says, "Tell you what—you don't say anything about the sheep, I won't say anything about the kid."

Can You Pray?
As the storm raged, Captain Logan of the HMS Waver realized his ship was going down fast. He shouted out, "Who here knows how to pray?" One crew member stepped forward. "Yes, Captain, I know how to pray." "Good Mate," said the captain, "you pray while the rest of us put on our life jackets—we're one short."

A drunk swaggers out of a bar and bumps into a nun. He steps back and then punches her right in the face, knocking her to the ground. She is so shocked that she does nothing except tries to stand as he hits her again. This time she falls down again and he kicks her in the butt. Then he picks her up and throws her into the wall, puts his face up to hers and says, "Not so tough NOW, are you, Batman?"

THE BEER PRAYER – Our lager,
Which art in barrels,
Hallowed be thy ale,
Thy will be drunked, (I will be
drunked),
At home as I am in d'tavern.
Give us this day our foamy head,
And forgive us our splashes,
As we forgive those who splashed
against us,
And lead us not to incarceration,
But deliver us from hangovers,
For thine is the beer,
The bitterest and the lager,
Forever and shall there be,Barmen

Religious Ancient Writings of Israel A team of archaeologists was excavating in Israel when they came upon a cave. Written on the wall of the cave were the following symbols in order of appearance:

1. A female symbol
2. A Mule
3. A shovel
4. A fish
5. A Star of David

They decided that this was a unique find and the writings were at least more than three thousand years old. They chopped out the piece of stone and had it brought to the museum where archaeologists from all over the world came to carefully study the ancient symbols. They held a huge meeting after months of conferences to discuss what they could agree was the meaning of the markings. (The President of their society stood up and pointed at the first drawing and said: "This looks like a woman. We can judge that this race was family oriented and held women in high esteem. You can also tell they were intelligent, as the next symbol resembles a donkey, so, they were smart enough to have animals help them till the soil. The next drawing looks like a shovel of some sort, which means they even had tools to help them. Even further proof of their high intelligence is the fish, which means that if they had a famine hit the earth, whereby the food didn't grow, they would take to the sea for food. The last symbol appears to be the Star of David which means they were evidently Hebrews." The audience applauded enthusiastically and the President smiled and said, "I'm glad to see that you are all in full agreement with our interpretations." Suddenly a little old man stood up in the back of the room and said, "I object to every word. The explanation of what the writings say is quite simple. First of all, everyone knows that Hebrews don't read from left to right, but from right to left...Now, look again..." It now says: "'Holy Mackerel, Dig The Ass On That Bitch!'

A preacher visits an elderly woman from his congregation. As he sits on the couch he notices a small bowl of peanuts on the coffee table. "Mind if I have a few?" he asks. "Be my guest," the woman replies. They chat for over an hour and as the preacher stands to leave, he realizes instead of eating just a few peanuts, he has emptied the bowl. Oh my, did I do that?" asks the priest, as he points to the emptied bowl of peanuts.

That's all right," the woman replied. "Ever since I lost my dentures, all I can do is suck off the chocolate."

— — — — — — — — — —

Father Peter and His New Suit

For Father's Peter's 60th birthday, the congregation at St Mary's, Newark, New Jersey decided to give him a present of a new suit.

Father Peter was so moved by the gift that the following Sunday he stood before everyone and began his homily with a tear in his eye, 'Today I am preaching to you in my birthday suit.'

What the Pope really said...

A Swiss Financier was in Rome on a business trip. Being that he was Catholic, he wanted to see the Pope. He went to the Vatican and waited in a long procession of faithfuls for a long time. Finally the Pope emerged and proceeded down the line. The Swiss Financier was wearing his finest Hugo Boss suit and Italian loafers, and was hoping that the Pope would notice him. To his disappointment, however, the Pope went straight past him without so much as a glance. The financier was even further dismayed when a few meters further down the line, the Pope stopped in front of a decrepit local hobo, leant forward and said a few words into the hobo's ear.

Straight afterwards the Swiss financier man approached the hobo, and offered to trade his fine Hugo Boss suit for the Hobo's shabby outfit including a bottle a booze covered in a brown paper bag. The hobo readily agreed. The next day the Swiss Financier went back to the Vatican wearing the vagrant's gear, to all intents and purposes looking (and smelling) like a homeless drunk bum. He waited in the line again until the Pope emerged and proceeded down the line. This time the Pope noticed him immediately, came straight towards him, leant forward and

whispered in his ear: "Fuckin drunkard, I thought
I told you to fuck off! "

— — — — — — — — — — —

Misspelled?

In an ancient monastery of d'Medici, a new monk
arrived to join his brothers in copying books and
scrolls in the monastery's scriptorium. He was
assigned as a rubricator on copies of text that had
already been transcribed by hand. One day he
asked Father Gino (the head and most holy
curator of the Scriptorium), " Father, does not the
copying by hand of other copies allow for
monumental chances of error? How do we know
we are not copying the mistakes of someone else?
Are they ever checked against the original text?"
"A very good point, my son," said Father Gino.
"I will take one of the latest bound copies down
to the vault and compare it to the original text."
Father Gino went down to the vault and began his
verification. After a day had passed, the monks
began to worry and went down looking for the
old priest. As they approached the vault, they
heard sobbing and crying. When they opened the
door, they found Fr. Gino sobbing over the new
copy and the original leather-bound fragile text,
both open before him on the table. "Reverend
Father, what is wrong?" asked one of the monks.
"Oh, my God," sobbed the priest, "the word is
'celebrate!'"

— — — — — — — — — — —

A nun and a priest

A Nun and a Priest were crossing the Sahara
Desert on a camel. On the fiftieth day out the
camel suddenly dropped dead without warning.
After dusting themselves off, the nun and the
priest assessed their situation. After a long period
of silence, the priest spoke. "Well sister this looks
pretty grim." "I know father." The nun answered.
"In fact," said the priest, "I don't think it will be
likely that we can survive more than a day or
two." "I agree." said the nun. "Sister, since we
are unlikely to make it out of here alive would
you do me a favor? "Anything Father." "I've
never seen a woman's tits before. Would you
show me yours?" "Well under the circum stances
I don't see it being a problem." The nun opened
her habit and the priest enjoyed the sight of her
sagging breast. "Father, could I ask some thing of
you?" "Yes Sister," "I have never seen a man's
dick Could I see yours?" "I suppose that would
be OK," the priest replied and lifted his robe. "Oh
father, can I touch it?"
This the priest allowed and soon his dick became
hard. "Sister, you know if I put this in the right
place it can give life?" "Is that so?" replied the
nun "Yes it is sister." "Then stick it up the camels
arse, give IT some life, and lets get the fuck out
of here."

— — — — — — — — — —

A REALLY WISE PRIEST

A woman starts dating a married doctor. Before too long, she becomes pregnant and they don't know what to do. About nine months later, just about the time she is going to give birth, a priest goes into the hospital for an enlarged prostate. The doctor says to the woman, "I have a plan. After I've operated on the priest, I'll give the baby to him and tell him it was a miracle." So, the doctor delivers the baby and then operates on the priest.

After the operation he goes in to the priest and says, "Father, you're not going to believe what I found in you! "What?" says the priest. "What could it be?" "You gave birth to a child." "But that's impossible!" "I just did the operation," insists the doctor. "It's a miracle! And, he presents the priest with a bouncing baby boy. "Here's your baby." Fifteen years later, the priest realizes he must tell his son the truth. So, he sits the boy down and says, "Son, I have something to tell you. I'm not your father."
The son says, "What do you mean, you're not my father?" The priest replies, "I'm your mother. The cardinal is your father."

———————————

A Tax Official has come to a rural synagogue for their first audit ever. The nervous rabbi is accompanying him. "Rabbi, tell me, please, after you have distributed all your unleavened bread, what do you do with the crumbs?" "Well my goi, we gather them carefully and send them to the city and then they make bread of them again and send it to us." "Ah. So what about candles after they are burnt? What do you do with the ends?" "We send them to the city as well, and they make new candles from them and send them to us." "And what about circumcision? What do you do with those leftover pieces?" The rabbi, wearily, replies, "We send them to the city as well." "To the city!? And what do they send to you?" The rabbi looks at him with a puzzled look on his face. "Today they have sent you to us. No?" ask the rabbi.

———————————

Unitarian-Universalists are the only religious group that refer to their deity in the heavens as "To whom it may concern"

————————————

"Who Enters Heaven?"
A minister dies and is waiting in line at the Pearly
Gates of heaven. Ahead of him is a guy of middle
eastern descent who's dressed in sunglasses, a
loud shirt, and shorts. Saint Peter addresses this
guy, "Who are you, so that I may know whether
or not to admit you to the Kingdom of Heaven?"
The guy replies, "I'm Abdul, a New York City
taxi-driver." Saint Peter consults his list. He
smiles and says to the taxi-driver, "Go right on
in." The taxi-driver goes into Heaven and it's the
minister's turn. He stands erect and booms out, "I
am Father Floria, pastor of God's people in
Levittsville, New Hampshire for the last forty-
three years." Saint Peter consults his list. He says
to the minister, "I'm sorry but we are full of
pastors. You'll have to wait." "Just a minute,"
says the minister. "That man was a taxi-driver
and he gets into the gates of heaven. How can
this be?" "Up here, we work by results," says
Saint Peter. "While you preached, people slept;
while he drove, people prayed."

————————————

What do you get if you cross a Seventh-Day
Adventist and an agnostic?
Someone who knocks on your door at 8:00 AM
on a Saturday and has no idea why.

————————————

Two elderly nuns were asked to paint a room in
the town orphanage, and the last instruction of
the Mother Superior, before leaving to do the job,

is that they must not get even a drop of paint on their habits. After conferring about this for a while, the two nuns decide to lock the door of the room, strip off their habits, and paint in the nude. In the middle of the project, there comes a knock at the door. "Who is it?", calls one of the nuns. "Blind man," replies a voice from the other side of the door. The two nuns look at each other and shrug, and, deciding that no harm can come from letting a blind man into the room, they open the door. "Nice tits," says the man, "where do you want these blinds?"

————————————

Three nuns were talking. The first nun said, "I was cleaning in Father's room the other day and do you know what I found? A bunch of porno graphic magazines and videos." "What did you do?" the other nuns asked. "Well, of course I removed them and dipped them in holy water then threw them in the trash." The second nun said, "Well, I can top that. I was in Father's room the other day, too. I found a bunch of condoms!" "Oh my!" gasped the other nuns. "What did you do?" they asked. "I took them, dipped them in holy water and poked holes in all of them the put them back!" she replied. BOOM! The third nun fainted.

Two elderly nuns, Sister Ignatius and Sister Bonitus, are traveling through Europe in their rental car. As they pass through Transylvania, a diminutive Dracula jumps onto the hood of the car and hisses through the windshield.

"Quick, quick!" shouts Sister Ignatius. "What shall we do?" "Drive faster" replied Sister Bonitus. So Sister Ignatius drives faster but the Dracula doesn't budge. "What now?" cried Sister Ignatius. "Turn the windshield wipers on. That will get rid of the abomination," says Sister Bonitus. Sister Ignatius switches them on, knocking Dracula about, but he clings on and continues hissing at the nuns. "What shall I do now?" she shouts. "Switch on the windshield washer. I filled it up with Holy Water before we left," says Sister Bonitus. Sister Ignatius turns on the windshield washer. Dracula screams as the water burns him, but he still clings on and continues hissing at the nuns. "Now what?" shouts Sister Ignatius. "Show him your cross," says Sister Bonitus. "Now you're talking," says Sister Ignatius as she opens the window and shouts, "Get your fucking ass off our rent-a-car!"

— — — — — — — — — — —

Two nuns went out of the convent to sell cookies. One of them is known as Sister Time (ST) and the other one is known as Sister Logical (SL). It is getting dark and they are still far away from the convent: SL: Have you noticed that man has been following us for the past half-hour?

ST: Yes, I wonder what he wants.

SL: It's logical. He wants to rape us.

ST: Oh, no! At this rate he will reach us in 15 minutes at the most. What can we do?

SL: The only logical thing to do of course is that we have to start walking faster. ST: It is not working.

SL: Of course it is not working. The man did the only obvious thing to do, he walked faster, too.

ST: So, what shall we do? At this rate he will reach us in one minute.

SL: The only logical thing we can do is split. You go that way and I'll go this way. He cannot follow both of us. So the man decided to go after Sister Logical. Sister Time arrives at the convent and is worried because Sister Logical has not yet arrived. Finally, Sister Logical arrives.

ST: Sister Logical! Thank God you are here! Tell us what happened!

SL: The only logical thing happened. The man could not follow both of us, so he followed me.

ST: So, what happened? Please tell us.

SL: The only logical thing. I started to run as fast as I could.

ST: So what happened?

SL: The man also started to run as fast as he could.

ST: And what else? SL: He reached me.

ST: Oh, no! What did you do then?

SL: The only logical thing to do. I lifted my dress up.
ST: Oh, Sister. What did the man do?
SL: The only logical thing to do. He pulled down his pants.
ST: Oh, no! What happened then?
SL: Isn't it logical, Sister? A nun with her dress up can run faster than a man with his pants down.
(Oh, and you thought it was a dirty joke..hehehehehe)

———————————

A rabbi, a priest and a minister walk into a bar.

The bartender looks up and says, 'What is this, a joke?'

Chapter 2. - MEN, WOMEN, HUSBANDS, AND WIVES

— — — — — — — —

Men and Women

Two guys and a woman were sitting at a bar talking about their professions. The one guy says, "I'm a Y.U.P.P.I.E., ya know...Young, Urban, Professional. The second guy says "I'm a D.I.N.K., ya know, Double Income No Kids." They asked the woman, "What are you?" She replied...."I'm a W.I.F.E., ya know, Wash, Iron, Fuck, Etc."

— — — — — — — —

Two bored casino dealers are waiting at the crap table. A very attractive
blonde woman from Alabama arrived and bet twenty-thousand dollars
($20,000) on a single roll of the dice. She said, "I hope you don't mind,
but I feel much luckier when I play topless." With that, she stripped to the waist, rolled the dice and yelled, "Come on
baby! Alabama Girl needs new clothes!" As the dice came to a stop, she jumped up-and-down and squealed,
"YES! YES! I WON! I WON!"
She hugged each of the dealers then picked up her winnings and her clothes,
and quickly departed. The dealers stared at each other dumbfounded.

Finally, one of them asked, "What did she roll?"
The other answered, "I don't know. I thought you were watching."
Moral:
Not all Southerners are stupid.
Not all blondish women are dumb.
But, all men..... are men.

A man feared his wife wasn't hearing as well as she used to and he thought she might need a hearing aid. Not quite sure how to approach her, he called the family Doctor to discuss the problem.
The Doctor told him there is a simple informal test the husband could perform to give the Doctor a better idea about her hearing loss.
Here's what you do," said the Doctor, "stand about 40 feet away from her, and in a normal conversational speaking tone see if she hears you.
If not, go to 30 feet, then 20 feet, and so on until you get a response."
That evening, the wife is in the kitchen cooking dinner, and he was in the den.
He says to himself, "I'm about 40 feet away, let's see what happens.

Then in a normal tone he asks, 'Honey, what's for dinner?"
No response.
So the husband moves closer to the kitchen, about 30 feet from his
wife and repeats "Honey, what's for dinner?"
Still no response.
Next he moves into the dining room where he is about 20 feet from his
wife and asks, "Honey, what's for dinner?"
Again he gets no response.
So, he walks up to the kitchen door, about 10 feet away.
"Honey, what's for dinner?" Again there is no response.
So he walks right up behind her. "Honey, what's for dinner?" (I just love this)
"Ralph , for the FIFTH time, CHICKEN!"

Gifts from God Seems God was just about done creating the universe, but he had two extra things left in his bag of tricks, so he decided to split them between Adam and Eve. He told the couple that one of the things he had to give away was the ability to pee with a penis. It's a very handy thing since you can even urinate standing up, God told the couple, who he found under an apple tree. "I was wondering if either one of you wanted that ability." Adam jumped up and blurted, "Oh, give that to me! I'd love to be able to do that! It seems a sort of thing a man should do. Oh please, oh please, oh please, let me have that ability. It'd be so great!" "When I'm working in the garden or naming the animals, I could just stand there and let it fly. It'd be so cool. I could pee with no hands. Oh please God, let it be me who you give that gift to, let me stand and pee, oh please......" On and on he went like an excited little boy who had to pee. Eve just smiled and told God that if Adam really wanted that so badly, then he should have it. It seemed to be the sort of thing that would make him happy, and she really wouldn't mind if Adam were the one given this ability. And so Adam was given the ability to control the direction of his misdirection while in a vertical position. He was happy and did celebrate by wetting down the bark on the tree nearest him, laughing with delight all the while. And it was good. " Fine," God said, looking back into his bag of leftover gifts. "What's left here? Oh yes, multiple orgasms....."

A couple had been married 27 years. One afternoon they were working in the garden together. As the wife was bending over pulling weeds, the husband said, "Honey, every year your butt just gets bigger and bigger. I bet it is as big as the BBQ grill now." The husband, feeling he needed to prove his point, got a yardstick, measured the grill & then measured his wife's butt. "Yep, he said, 'Just what I thought, just about the same size!" Angrily, she storms inside & didn't speak to her husband the rest of the day. That evening when they went to bed, the husband cuddled up to his wife and said, "How about it honey?" How about a little sex?" The wife rolled over & turned her back to him, giving him the cold shoulder. "What's the matter?" he asked. To which she replied, "You don't think I am going to fire up my big ass grill for one little wiener, do you?"

Woman's famous words of wisdom:
Friends don't let friends take home ugly men
…and the men's words (no wisdom)
Don't trust anything that bleeds for 5 days and doesn't die.

Alice and Bob were living at a nursing home and had been carrying on a love affair for 20 years. They were both 102 years old and wheelchair bound. Every night, they would meet in the music room. Alice would passively hold Bob's penis, and they would sing for an hour or so. It wasn't much, but it was all they had. One night Bob didn't show up. He didn't show up for the next two nights either. Alice assumed he was dead, but then she saw him happily wheeling about the grounds. She confronted him and said, "Where were you these past couple of nights?"

He replied, "If you must know, I was with another woman." "Bastard!" she cried. "What were you doing?" "We do the exact same thing that you and I do," he replied. "Is she prettier or younger than I am?" she asked. "Nope, she looks the same, and she is 107 years old." "Well then, what does she have that I don't?" Alice asked. Bob smiled and said, "Parkinson's."

It's a beautiful warm summer day and a man and his wife are at the zoo. The husband notices his wife is wearing a beautiful fragrance. So, he reaches over and asked if she'd like to sneak around the back of the zoo cages and have sex. No, she replied, I have a headache. As they walk through the ape exhibit and pass in front of a very large gorilla, the gorilla catches scent of the young wife and goes ape. He jumps up on the bars, holding on with one hand (and 2 feet), grunting and pounding his chest with the free hand. He is obviously excited about this fragrant lady.

The husband, noticing the excitement, suggests that his wife tease the poor fellow. The husband suggests she pucker her lips, wiggle her bottom and play along. She does and Mr. Gorilla gets even more excited, making noises that would wake the dead. Then the husband suggests that she let one of her straps fall. She does, and Mr. Gorilla is just about to tear the bars down. "Now try lifting your dress up your thighs." This drives the gorilla absolutely crazy. Then, quickly the husband grabs his wife by the hair, rips open the door to the cage, slings her in with the gorilla and says, "Now, tell HIM you have a headache."

_____

Woman's Quote of the Day:
"Men are like fine wine. They all start out like grapes, and it's our job to crush the life essence out of them and keep them in the dark until they mature into something you'd like to have dinner with."

Man's Quote of the Day:
"Women are like fine wine. They all start out fresh, flavorful and intoxicating to the mind and then turn full-bodied with age until they go all sour and vinegary and give you a headache."

Sometimes, email is a wonderful thing
As you are receiving this note by e-mail, it's
wise to remember how easily this wonderful
technology can be misused, sometimes
unintentionally, with serious consequences.
Like this true story (NOT!): Consider the
case of the Washington State man who left
the rain soaked streets of Seattle for a
vacation in Florida. His wife was on a
business trip and was planning to meet him
there the next day. When he reached his
hotel, he decided to send his wife a quick e-
mail. Unable to find the scrap of paper on
which he had written her e-mail address, he
did his best to type it in from memory.
Unfortunately, he missed one letter, and his
note was directed instead to an elderly
preacher's wife, whose husband had passed
away only the day before. When the grieving
widow checked here-mail, she took one look
at the monitor, let out a piercing scream, and
fell to the floor in a dead faint. At the sound,
her family rushed into the room and saw this
note on the screen: Dearest Wife, Just got
checked in. Everything prepared for your
arrival tomorrow. P.S. Hell, it's really hot
here.

WOMEN'S Unabridged ENGLISH DICTIONARY:

Yes = No

No = Yes

Maybe = No

I'm sorry = You'll be sorry

We need = I want It's your decision = The correct decision should be obvious by now

Do what you want = You'll pay for this later

We need to talk = I need to complain

Sure…go ahead = I don't want you to

I'm not upset = Of course I'm upset, you moron!

You're …so manly = You need a shave and you sweat a lot

You're certainly attentive tonight = Is sex all you ever think about??

Be romantic, turn out the lights = I have flabby thighs

Do you love me? = I'm going to ask for something expensive

How much do you love me? = I did something today that you're really not going to like

I'll be ready in a minute = Kick off your shoes and find a good game on TV

Is my butt fat? = Tell me I'm beautiful

You have to learn to communicate = Just agree with me

Are you listening to me?? = Too late, you're dead

MEN'S Unabridged ENGLISH DICTIONARY:

I'm hungry = I'm hungry

I'm sleepy = I'm sleepy

I'm tired = I'm tired

Do you want to go to a movie? = I'd eventually like to have sex with you

Can I take you out to dinner? = I'd eventually like to have sex with you

Can I call you sometime? = I'd eventually like to have sex with you

May I have this dance? = I'd eventually like to have sex with you

Nice dress = Nice cleavage!

You look tense, let me give you a massage = I want to fondle you

What's wrong? = I guess sex tonight is out of the question

I'm bored = Do you want to have sex?

I love you = Let's have sex now

I love you, too = Okay, I said it…we'd better have sex now!

Will you marry me? = I want to make it illegal for you to have sex with other guys

---

Is it Love, Lust and Marriage? You decide.

LOVE When your eyes meet across a crowded room.
LUST When your tongues meet across a crowded room.
MARRIAGE When you try to lose your spouse in a crowded room.

LOVE When you share everything you own.
LUST When you steal everything they own.
MARRIAGE When the bank owns everything.

LOVE When you phone each other just to say, "Hi."
LUST When you phone each other to pick a hotel room.
MARRIAGE When you phone each other to bitch about work.

LOVE When you write poems about your partner.
LUST When all you write is your phone number.
MARRIAGE When all you write is checks.

LOVE When your only concern is for your partner's feelings.

LUST When your only concern is to find a room with mirrors all around.
MARRIAGE When you're only concerned as to what's on TV.

LOVE When you are proud to be seen in public with your partner.
LUST When you only see each other naked.
MARRIAGE When you never see each other awake.

LOVE When all the songs on the radio describe exactly how you feel.
LUST When the song on the radio determines how you do it.
MARRIAGE When you listen to talk radio.

LOVE When breaking up is something you try not to think about.
LUST When staying together is something you try not to think about.

MARRIAGE When just getting through the day is your only thought.
LOVE When you're only interested in doing things with your partner.
LUST When you're only interested in doing things TO your partner.
MARRIAGE When you're only interested in your golf score.

(NOTE...Based upon this test, the author just likes his partner)

MEN ARE

Men are like...Coffee The best ones are rich, warm, and can keep you up all night long.

Men are like...Bananas. The older they get, the less firm they are.

Men are like...Bank Machines. Once they withdraw, they lose interest.

Men are like...Blenders. You need one, but not every day.

Men are like...Commercials. You can't believe a word they say.

Men are like...Computers. Hard to figure out and never have enough memory.

Men are like...Coolers. Load them with beer and you can take them anywhere.

Men are like...Copiers. You need them for reproduction, but that's about it.

Men are like...Government bonds. They take so long to mature.

Men are like...Horoscopes. They always tell you what to do and are usually wrong.

Men are like...Lawn Mowers. If you're not pushing one around, then you're riding it.

Men are like...Lava lamps. Fun to look at, but not all that bright.

Men are like...Mascara. They usually run at the first sign of emotion.

Men are like…Mini skirts. If you're not careful, they'll creep up your legs.

Men are like…Chinese Food. They satisfy you, but only for a little while.

Men are like…Place mats. They only show up when there's food on the table.

Men are like…Used Cars. Both are easy-to-get, cheap, and unreliable.

Men are like…Vacations. They never seem to be long enough.

Men are like…Snowstorms. You never know when they're coming, how many inches you'll get or how long they will last.

A man and a woman were married for 31 years. When they first got married the man said, "I am putting a box under the bed. You must promise never to look in it." In all their 31 years of marriage the woman never looked. However, on the afternoon of their 31st anniversary, curiosity got the best of her and she lifted the lid and peeked inside. In the box were 5 empty beer bottles and $1762.15 in small bills and change. She closed the box and put it back under the bed. Now that she knew what was in the box, she was doubly curious as to why. That evening they were out at a special dinner at their favorite restaurant. After dinner the woman could no longer contain her curiosity and she confessed saying, "I am so sorry. For all these years I kept my promise and never looked. However, today the temptation was too much and I gave in. But now I need to know why do you keep the bottles in the box?" The man thought for a while and said, "I guess after all these wonderful years you deserve to know the truth." "Whenever I was unfaithful to you I put an empty beer bottle in the box under the bed to remind myself not to do it again." The woman was shocked but said, "I am very disappointed and saddened but I guess after all those years away from home on the road, temptation does happen and I guess 5 times is not that bad considering the years." They hugged and made their peace. A little while later the woman asked the man, "Why do you have all that money in the box?" To which the man answered, "Whenever the box filled with empties, I cashed them in."

THE GOOD, THE BAD, AND THE UGLY
(and we don't mean the movie!)

Good: Your hubby and you agree, no more kids
Bad: You can't find your birth control pills
Ugly: Your daughter borrowed them

Good: Your son studies a lot in his room
Bad: You find several porn movies hidden there
Ugly: You're in them

Good: Your husband understands fashion
Bad: He's a cross-dresser
Ugly: He looks better than you

Good: Your son's finally maturing
Bad: He's involved with the woman next door
Ugly: So are you

Good: You give the birds and bees talk to your daughter
Bad: She keeps interrupting
Ugly: With corrections

Good: Your wife's not talking to you
Bad: She wants a divorce
Ugly: She's a lawyer

Good: The postman's early
Bad: He's wearing fatigues and carrying an AK47
Ugly: You gave him nothing for Christmas

Good: Your daughter got a new job
Bad: As a hooker
Ugly: Your coworkers are her best clients
Way ugly: She makes more money than you do.

Good: Your son is dating someone new
Bad: It's another man
Ugly: He's your best friend

A woman was in bed with her lover when she heard her husband opening the front door. "Hurry!" she said, "stand in the corner." She quickly rubbed baby oil all over him and then she dusted him with talcum powder. "Don't move until I tell you to," she whispered. "Just pretend you're a statue." "What's this, honey?" the husband inquired as he entered the room. "Oh, it's just a statue I bought at IKEA," she replied, lying nonchalantly. "The Smiths bought one for their bedroom. I liked it so much, I got one for us too." No more was said about the statue, not even later that night when they went to sleep. Around two in the morning the husband got out of bed, went to the kitchen and returned a while later with a sandwich and a glass of milk. "Here," he said to the 'statue', "eat something. I stood like an idiot at the Smiths for three days and nobody offered me as much as a glass of water."

(Moral: *IKEA DOES GOOD BUSI NESS*.....hehehehehehe)

HOW TO ATM (man's version)

Pull up to ATM
Insert card
Enter PIN number
Take cash, card, and receipt
Drive away

HOW TO ATM (woman's version)

Pull up to ATM
Back up and pull forward to get closer
Shut off engine
Put keys in purse
Get out of car because you're too far from machine
Hunt for card in purse
Insert card
Locate grocery receipt in purse with PIN #
Enter PIN
Study instructions for at least 2 minutes
Hit "cancel"
Reenter correct PIN #
Check balance
Look for envelope
Go through purse for ink pen
Make out deposit slip
Study instructions again

Endorse check 19. Make deposit
Make cash withdrawal
Get back into car
Check makeup in mirror
Look for keys in purse S
tart car
Check makeup again Start pulling away from
ATM Stop Back up to machine Get out of car
Retrieve card and receipt Get back into car
Put card in wallet Put receipt in checkbook
Enter deposit and withdrawal into checkbook
Clear space in purse for wallet and
checkbook Check makeup Put car in reverse
38. Put car in drive. Drive away from
machine 40. Drive 3 miles down the road
release the parking brake!

———————————————

You know your town is too small….

A girl asks her boyfriend to come over Friday night and have dinner with her parents. Since this is such a big event, the girl announces to her boyfriend that after dinner, she would like to go out and have sex for the first time. Well, the boy is ecstatic, but he has never had sex before, so he takes a trip to the pharmacist to get some condoms. The local pharmacist helps the boy for about an hour. He tells the boy everything there is to know about condoms and sex. At the register, the local pharmacist asks the boy how many condoms. He'd like to buy 100 condoms. The pharmacist thinks to himself the guy is really gonna give it to her! That night, the boy shows up at the girl's parent's house and meets his girl friend at the door. "Oh, I'm so excited for you to meet my parents. Come on in!" The boy goes inside and is taken to the dinner table where the girl's parents are seated. The boy quickly offers to say grace and bows his head. A minute passes, and the boy is still in deep prayer with his head down. 10 minutes pass, and still no movement from the boy.
Finally, after 20 minutes with his head down, the girlfriend finally leans over and whispers

to the boyfriend, "I had no idea you were this religious." The boy turns and whispers back, "I had no idea your father was our pharmacist…"

A FEW SIMPLE SUGGESTIONS ON HOW TO SATISFY A WOMAN
Lick, paw, ogle, caress, praise, pamper, relish, savor, massage, empathize, serenade, compliment, support, dig, feed, laminate, tantalize, bathe, humor, placate, stimulate, jiffylube, stroke, console, bark, purr, hug, baste, marinate, coddle, excite, pacify, tattoo, protect, phone, correspond, anticipate, nuzzle, smooch, toast, minister to, for give, sacrifice, ply, accessorize, leave, return, beseech, sublimate, entertain, charm, lug, drag, crawl, tunnel, show equality for, spackle, oblige, fascinate, attend, implore, bawl, shower, shave, ululate, trust, dip, twirl, dive, grovel, ignore, defend, serve, rub, rib, salve, bite, taste, nibble, gratify, take her to Funky town, scuttle like a crab on the ocean floor of her existence, diddle, doodle, hokey-pokey, hanky-panky, crystal blue persuasion, flip, flop, fly, don't care if I die, swing, slip, slide, slather, mollycoddle, squeeze, moisturize, humidify, lather, tingle, slam-dunk, keep on rockin' in the free world, wet,

slicken, undulate, gelatinize, brush, tingle, dribble, drip, dry, knead, fluff, fold, blue-coral wax, ingratiate, indulge wow, dazzle, amaze, flabbergast, enchant, idolize and worship, and then go back and do it again.

———————————

HOW TO SATISFY A MAN EVERY TIME:

a good Blow job

Once upon a time, a perfect man and a perfect woman met. After a perfect courtship, they had a perfect wedding. Their life together was, of course, perfect. One snowy, stormy Christmas Eve, this perfect couple was driving their perfect car (a Range Rover) along a winding road, when they noticed someone at the side of the road in distress. Being the perfect couple, they stopped to help. There stood Santa with a huge bundle of gifts. Not wanting to disappoint any children on the eve of Christmas, the perfect couple loaded Santa and his gifts into their vehicle. Soon they were driving along delivering the gifts. Unfortunately, the driving conditions deteriorated and the perfect couple and Santa Claus had an accident. Only one of them survived the accident. Who was the survivor? (next page)

The perfect woman. She's the only one who really existed in the first place. Everyone knows there is no Santa Claus and there is no such thing as a perfect man. (Women, SKIP the next page. Men, turn the page)

So, if there is no perfect man and no Santa Claus, the perfect woman must have been driving. This explains why there was a car accident. And, by the way, if you're a woman and you're reading this, this brings up another point: women never listen either.

CATS AND DOGS (I think a woman wrote this)

CATS & DOGS What Is a Cat?
Cats do what they want.
They rarely listen to you.
They're totally unpredictable.
They whine when they are not happy.
When you want to play, they want to be alone.
When you want to be alone, they want to play.
They expect you to cater to their every whim.
They're moody.
They leave hair everywhere.
They drive you nuts and cost an arm and a leg. Conclusion: They're tiny women in cheap fur coats.

_____

What Is a Dog?

Dogs lie around all day, sprawled on the most comfortable piece of furniture in the house.

They can hear a package of food opening half a block away, but don't hear you when you're in the same room.

They can look dumb and lovable all at the same time.

They growl when they are not happy.

When you want to play, they want to play. When you want to be alone, they want to play.

They are great at begging.

They will love you forever if you rub their tummies.

They leave their toys everywhere.

They do disgusting things with their mouths and then try to give you a kiss. Conclusion: They're tiny men in cheap little fur coats.

_____

Men and Women

The patient's family gathered to hear what Dr. Frankenstein had to say. "Things don't look good. The only chance is a brain transplant. This is an experimental procedure. It might work, but the bad news is that brains are very expensive, and you will have to pay the costs yourselves." "Well, how much does a brain cost?" asked the relatives. "For a male brain, $500,000. For a female brain, $200,000." Some of the younger male relatives tried to look shocked, but all the men nodded because they thought they under stood. But the patient's daughter was unsatisfied and asked: "Why the difference in price between male brains and female brains?" "A standard pricing practice," said the head of the team. "Women's brains have to be marked down because they have actually been used."

———————————————

The Different Types of Boyfriends

Joe Sensitive—"After I wash the dishes, let's cuddle, OK?" Also known as: Mr. Nice Guy, Family man, Honey, Darling, Soft-boiled Egg, Snuggle pup
Advantages: Well-behaved; irons own shirts
Disadvantages: Irritatingly compassionate, wimpy

Mr. Cheapy—"We'll go dutch, OK?" Also known as: Mr. Tightass, penny pincher, blue balls Advantages: always has change
Disadvantages: Never lends it to you .

Old Man Grumpus—"People are stupid. The world can go to hell. Let's stay home and watch TV." Also known as: Grumbles, Sour puss, Stick-in the-mud, Old Fogey, Slow Mover, Jerk
Advantages: Stays put; predictable
Disadvantages: Royal pain in the ass

Flinchy—"I—I'm sorry for whatever it was I did." Also known as: Trembly, Creampuff, Hey you

Advantages: Jumps entertainingly when startled
Disadvantages: Easily spooked; surrenders without a struggle

Bigfoot—"Shut yer trap, I'm thinkin'." Also known as: Chunk-style, Lummox, Ignoramus, Galoot, the Hulk, Big 'n' Dumb
Advantages: Can tote bales; is easily fooled
Disadvantages: Can break you in half, sweats like a pig

Lazybones—"Zzzzzz" Also known as: Lucky Dog, Parasite, Bum, Sponge, Snoozebucket, Drug Addict
Advantages: Well rested; easy target
Disadvantages: Unlikely to fulfill your dreams

The Dreamer—"Someday I'm going to be rich and famous. I don't know how, but—"
Also known as: Struggling Artist, Philosopher, Buffoon, Bag of Wind
Advantages: Tells good stories
Disadvantages: Will turn into "Old Man Grumpus"

Mr. Right—"While the servants wash the dishes, let's make love like crazed weasels in my new yacht, ok?" Also known as: Mr. Perfect, Jim Dandy

Advantages: Answer to a woman's prayer

Disadvantages: Hunted to extinction.

The Different Types of Girlfriends

Ms. Nice Guy—"Tickets to the boxing match? Oh, darling, you shouldn't have!" Also known as: Whattaguy, Precious, one of the boys, My Main Squeeze, Doormat
Advantages: Cheerful, agreeable, kindly
Disadvantages: May wise up someday
Ms. Spend it Girl -"Did you get me anything? also known as: Ms. Gold-digger, Ms. I date octogenarians
Advantages: Always looks good
Disadvantages: Looks good at your expense

Ms. Sickly—"Oh, my head. My head. My feet. My cramps. My cellulite." Also known as: Whiner, Mewler, Grumpy
Advantages: Predictable, she's always sick in bed while you're looking for her replacement
Disadvantages: Contagious

Ms Bossy pants—"Stand up straight. Put on a different tie. Get a haircut. Change your job. Make some money. Don't give me that look." Also known as: Whipcracker, The Sarge, Ms. Know-it-all, Ball and Chain, Yes Mom

Advantages: Often right
Disadvantages: Often right, but so what?

Ms. Vaguely Dissatisfied—"I just can't
decide. Should I switch my career, goals,
home, and hair color?" Also known as: The
Fretter, Worrywart, Typical, Aw C'mon
Honey
Advantages: Easily soothed
Disadvantages: Even more easily perturbed

Ms Girl Gone Wild —"I've got an idea. Lez
get drunk an' make love on the front lawn. I
done it before. S'fun." Also known as: Fast
Girl, Freewheeler, Goodtime Charleena,
Passed Out
Advantages: More fun than a barrel of
monkeys
Disadvantages: Unreliable; drives off cliffs

Ms. Huffy Pants—"I see nothing humorous
in those silly cartoons you keep snickering
at." Also known as: No Fun, Humorless Prig,
Cold fish, Chilly Proposition, Iceberg, Snarly
Advantages: Your friends will feel sorry for
you
Disadvantages: You will have no friends

Ms. Woman from Mars—"I believe this interpretive dance will explain how I feel about our relation ship." Also known as: The Babbler, Spooky Girl, Screwball, Loony,
Advantages: Entertaining, unfathomable
Disadvantages: Will read her poetry aloud

Ms. Dreamgirl—"I am utterly content with you just the way you are, my handsome genius of a boyfriend. I think we must make love like crazed weasels now!" Also known as: Ms. Right, Goddess, Knockout, Perfection, Gorgeous
Advantages: Funny, intelligent, uninhibited
Disadvantages: Will have nothing to do with you.

_____

How to Shower Like a Woman:

Take off fourteen layers of clothing you put on this morning. Walk to bathroom wearing robe and towel on head. If you happen to see husband along the way, ignore juvenile "turban-head" jokes and run to bathroom. Look at womanly physique in the mirror and stick out stomach so as to complain about how fat you're getting. Turn on hot water only. Look for facecloth, arm cloth, leg cloth, long loofah, wide loofah, and pumice stone.7. Wash hair once with Cucumber and Lemon shampoo with 83 added vitamins.

Rinse hair. Condition your hair with Cucumber and Lemon conditioner enhanced with natural crocus oil. Leave on hair for fifteen minutes.

Wash face with crushed apricot facial scrub for ten minutes until red and raw.

Try to wash entire rest of body with Ginger Nut and Java Cake body-wash.

Complain bitterly when you realize that your husband has once gain been EATING your Ginger Nut and Java Cake body wash.

Rinse conditioner off hair (this takes at least fifteen minutes as you must make sure that all the conditioner has come off).

Debate shaving armpits and legs and decide that you can't be bothered.

Scream loudly when your husband flushes the toilet and you get a rush of cold water.
Turn hot water on full and rinse off.
Dry with a towel the size of a small African country.

How to Shower Like a Man:
Sit on the edge of the bed and take off the underwear you've been walking around the house in all morning. Leave them on the floor.
Walk to bathroom wearing a towel. If you see your wife along the way, flash her.
Look at your manly physique in the mirror. Pat your beer belly with affection as if it were a Great Achievement. Suck in your gut to see if you have pecs. (No)
Turn on the water. 5. Check for pecs again. (Still No) 6. Get in the shower.
Don't bother to look for a washcloth. (You don't use one.)
Spend 5 minutes soaping your body and rinse.
Spend 15 minutes washing your crotch and surrounding area.
Wash your butt.
Shampoo your hair, do not use conditioner.
Make a shampoo mohawk.

Open the door and look at yourself in the mirror, giggle.
Pee.
Rinse off and get out of the shower.
Pick up the towel and sniff it. If it smells okay, go ahead and dry off with it. If it doesn't smell okay, holler to your wife to find you a clean one.
Return to the bedroom wearing the towel, if you pass your wife, flash her.

Two golfers were being held up as the twosome of women in front of them whiffed shots, hunted for lost balls and stood over putts for what seemed like hours. "I'll ask if we can play through," Bill said as he strode toward the women. Twenty yards from the green, however, he turned on his heel and went back to where his companion was waiting. "Can't do it," he explained, sheepishly. "One of them's my wife and the other's my mistress!" "I'll ask," said Jim. He started off, only to turn and come back before reaching the green. "What's wrong?" Bill asked. ""One of them's my wife and the other's my mistress too!" Small world, isn't it?" A male whale and a female whale were swimming off the coast of Canada when they noticed a whaling ship. The male whale recognized it as the same ship that had harpooned his father many years earlier. He said to the female whale, "let us both swim under ship and blow our air hole at same time and it should cause ship to turn over and sink." They tried it and sure enough, the ship turned over and quickly sank. Soon however, the whales realized the sailors were swimming to the safety of the shore. The male whale was enraged that they were going to get away and told the female, "Let us swim after them and gobble them up before they reach the shore." At this point he realized the female was becoming reluctant to follow him. "Look," she said, "I went along with the blow job, but I absolutely refuse to swallow the seamen."

Men Vs. Women
TOP 10 THINGS MEN KNOW ABOUT
WOMEN:
1. Tits
2. Ass
3.
4.
5.
6.
7.
8.
9.
10.

Men and Woman-<u>MEN FIGHT BACK!</u>

How many men does it take to open a beer?
> None, it should be opened by the time
> she brings it.

_____

Why is a Laundromat a really bad place to
pick up a woman?
> Because a woman who can't even
> afford a washing machine will never
> be able to support you.

_____

Why do women have smaller feet than men?
> So they can stand closer to the
> kitchen sink.

_____

How do you fix a woman's watch?
> You don't. There's a clock on the
> stove!

_____

Why do men pass gas more than women?
> Because women won't shut up long
> enough to build up pressure.

_____

If your dog is barking at the back door and your wife is yelling at the front door, which one do you let in first?

The dog, of course, at least he'll shut up after you let him in.

A man inserted an 'ad' in the classified: "Wife wanted". Next day he received a hundred letters. They all said the same thing: "You can have mine."

The most effective way to remember your wife's birthday is to forget it once.

First guy (proudly): "My wife's an angel!"
Second guy: "You're lucky, mine's still alive."

How do most men define marriage? An expensive way to get laundry done for free.

Just think, if it weren't for marriage, men would go through life thinking they had no faults at all.

If you want your wife to listen and pay undivided attention to every word you say, talk in your sleep.

Then there was a man who said, "I never knew what real happiness was until I got married; and then it was too late."

A little boy asked his father, "Daddy, how much does it cost to get married?" And the father replied, "I don't know son, I'm still paying."

A guy is driving down the street. A cop pulls him over and says, "Sir, were you aware that your wife fell out of the car about a mile back?" The guy says, "Oh, thank God! I thought I went deaf."

A couple of women were playing golf one sunny Saturday morning. The first of the twosome teed off and watched in horror as her ball headed directly toward a foursome of men playing the next hole. Indeed, the ball hit one of the men, and he immediately clasped his hands together at his crotch, fell to the ground and proceeded to roll around in evident agony. The woman rushed down to the man and immediately began to apologize. She said, "Please allow me to help. I'm a physical therapist and I know I could relieve your pain if you'd allow." "Ummph, oooh, nnooo, I'll be all right…I'll be fine in a few minutes," he replied breathlessly as he remained in the fetal position still clasping his hands together at his crotch. But she persisted, and he finally allowed her to help him. She gently took his hands away and laid them to the side, she loosened his pants, and she put her hands inside. She began to massage him. She then asked him, "How does that feel?" To which he replied, "It feels great, but my thumb still hurts like hell."

Dear Tech Support,
This is my 2nd upgrade, I originally bought Boyfriend
5.1 but then decided to upgrade Fiancé 6.0.
Now, I upgraded from Fiancé 6.0 to Husband 1.0 and noticed that the new program began making unexpected changes to the accounting software, severely limiting access to wardrobe, flower, and jewelry applications that operated flawlessly under Fiancé 6.0. No mention of this phenomenon was included in the product brochure. In addition, Husband 1.0 uninstalls many other valuable pro-grams such as Dinner Dancing 7.5, Cruise Ship 2.3, and Opera Night 6.1 and installs new, undesirable programs such as Poker Night 1.3, Saturday Football 5.0, Golf 2.4 and Clutter Everywhere 4.5. Conversation 8.0 no longer runs, and invariably crashes the system. Under no circum stances will it run Diaper Changing 14.1 or Housecleaning 2.6. I've tried running Nagging 5.3 to fix Husband 1.0, but this all purpose utility is of limited effectiveness. Can you help please!!!!
* Thank You,
Jane-

_____

Dear Jane:
This is a very common problem women complain about, but is mostly due to a primary misconception. Many people upgrade from Fiancé 6.0 to Husband 1.0 with no idea that your originally purchase Boyfriend 5.0 Is merely an ENTERTAINMENT package. However, Husband 1.0 is an OPERATING SYSTEM and was designed by its creator to run as few applications as possible. Further, you cannot purge Husband 1.0 and return to Boyfriend 5.0 because Husband 1.0 is not designed to do this. Hidden operating files within your system would cause Boyfriend 5.0 to emulate Husband 1.0, so nothing is gained. It is impossible to uninstall, delete, or purge the program files from the system, once installed. Any new program files can only be installed once per year, as Husband 1.0 has severely limited memory. Error messages are common, and a normal part of Husband 1.0. In desperation to play some of their "old time" favorite applications, or to get new applications to work, some women have tried to re-install Fiancé 6.0, or install Husband 2.0. This is a wonderful feature of Husband 2.0, secretly installed by the parent company as an integral part of the operating system.

Husband 1.0 must assume ALL responsibility for ALL faults and problems, regardless of root cause. To activate this great feature enter the command "C:\I THOUGHT YOU LOVED ME." Sometimes Tears 6.2 must be run simultaneously while entering the command. Husband 1.0 should then run the applications Apologize 12.3 and...Flowers/Chocolates 7.8. TECH TIP! Avoid excessive use of this feature. Overuse can create additional and more serious GPFs, and ultimately YOU may have to give a C:\APOLOGIZE command before the system will return to normal operations. Overuse can also cause Husband 1.0 to default to Grumpy Silence 2.5, or worse yet, Beer 6.0. Beer 6.0 is a very bad program that causes Husband 1.0 to create Fat Belly files and SnoringLoudly.wav files that are very hard to delete. Save yourself some trouble by following this tech tip! Just remember! The system will run smoothly, and take the blame for all GPFs, but because of this fine feature it can only intermittently run all the applications Boyfriend 5.0 ran. Husband 1.0 is a great program, but it does have limited memory and cannot learn new applications quickly. Consider buying additional software to improve performance. I personally

recommend HotFood 3.0, Lingerie 5.3 and Patience 10.1. Used in conjunction, these utilities can really help keep Husband 1.0 running smoothly. After several years of use, Husband 1.0 will become familiar and you will find many valuable embedded features such as FixesBrokenThings 2.1, Snuggling 4.2 and BestFriend 7.6. A final word of caution! Do NOT, under any circumstances, install MotherInLaw 1.0. This is not a supported application, and will cause selective shut down of the operating system. Husband 1.0 will run only Fishing 9.4 and Hunting 5.2 until MotherInLaw 1.0 is uninstalled. I hope these notes have helped. Thank you for choosing to install Husband 1.0 and we here at Tech Support wish you the best of luck in coming years. We trust you will learn to fully enjoy this product! *
With Regards,
Tech Support

Chapter 3 - EMAIL BLONDISH JOKES

Dear 1001 Internet Joke Reader,
Since your author is possibly blonde (note to self, should ask
hairdresser). I'm tired of real blondes being called stupid! So,
these jokes will reveal the truth! We know who the dum (err
dumb) ones are.
Blondish (check the roots) Joke

TWO BLONDISHES (CHECK THE ROOTS) AND A PHOTOG RAPHER

Judi and her friend Jill decided to have their picture taken and went to the photographer. The process was totally new to Judi, so she kept asking Jill questions. "What's he doing now?" "He's going to pull down the backdrop." "What's he doing now?" " He's going to set up the camera." " What's he doing now?" "He's going to focus." "Focus? What!?" "Both of us?"

THE BLONDE AND GOD

A blonde wanted to go ice fishing. She'd seen many books on the subject and, finally getting all the necessary tools together, she made for the ice.

After positioning her comfy footstool, she started to make a circular cut in the ice. Suddenly, from the sky, a voice boomed,

"THERE ARE NO FISH UNDER THE ICE."

Startled, the blonde moved farther down the ice, poured a thermos of cappuccino and began to cut yet another hole. Again from the heavens the voice bellowed,

"THERE ARE NO FISH UNDER THE ICE."

The blonde, now worried, moved clear down to the opposite end of the ice. She set up her stool once more and tried again to cut her hole.

The voice came once more,

"THERE ARE NO FISH UNDER THE ICE."

She stopped, looked skyward, and asked,

"IS THAT YOU, GOD?"

The voice replied,

"NO, THIS IS THE MANAGER OF THE HOCKEY RINK"

Two blondishes (check the roots) decided to rob a bank together. The first blondish, Judy, plans the robbery and goes over the plan with the second blondish, Buffy, in great detail. The robbery begins. Judy drives up in front of the bank, stops the car and says to Buffy, "I want to make absolutely sure you understand the plan. You are supposed to be in and out of the bank in no more than three minutes with the cash. Do you understand the plan?" "Perfectly," said Buffy. Buffy goes in the bank while Judy waits in the getaway car. One minute passes…Two minutes pass….Seven minutes pass…and Judy is really stressing out. Finally, the bank doors burst open! And here comes Buffy. She's got a safe wrapped up in rope and is dragging it to the car. About the time she gets the safe in the trunk of the car, the bank doors burst open again with the security guard coming out. The guard's pants and underwear are down around his ankles while he is firing his weapon. As the gals are getting away, Judy says "You are such a blondish! I thought you under-stood the plan!" Buffy said, "I did...I did exactly what you said!" "No, you idiot," said Judy. "You got it all mixed up. I said tie up the GUARD and blow the SAFE!"

Christine the blondish (check the roots) was getting pretty desperate for money. She decided to go to the nicer, richer neighborhoods around town and look for odd jobs as a handy woman. The first house she came to, a man answered the door and told Christine, "Yeah, I have a job for you. How would you like to paint the porch?" "Sure that sounds great!" said Christine. "Well, how much do you want me to pay you?" asked the man. "Is fifty bucks all right?" Christine asked. "Yeah, great. You'll find the paint and ladders you'll need in the Garage." The man went back into his house to his wife who had been listening. "Fifty bucks! Does she know the porch goes all the way around the house?" asked the wife. "Well, she must, she was standing right on it!" her husband replied. About 45 minutes later, Christine knocked on the door. "I'm all finished," she told the surprised homeowner. The man was amazed. "You painted the whole porch?" "Yeah," Christine replied, "I even had some paint left, so I put on two coats!" The man reached into his wallet to pay Christine. "Oh, and by the way," said Christine, "That's not a Porch, it's a Ferrari."

BLONDISH JOKE
(*This is bad, but funny*)
A blondish (check the roots) went into a world wide message center to send a message to her mother overseas. When the man told her it would cost $300 she exclaimed, "I don't have that kind of money!! But I would do ANYTHING to get a message to my mother in Poland!" The man arched an eyebrow. "Anything?" "Yes, anything" the blondish promised. With that, the man said, "Follow me." He walked into the next room and ordered, "Come in and close the door." She did. He then said, "Get on your knees."

She did. Then he said, "Take down my zipper." She did. He said, "Go ahead...take it out." She took it out and grabbed hold of it with both hands. The man closed his eyes and whispered, "Well....go ahead!"
The blondish slowly brought her lips closer, and while holding it close to her lips she said loudly "HELLO.....MOM???"

Stranded
Bill Gates is stranded on a desert island all alone for ten years. One day he sees a speck on the horizon. He thinks to himself, "It's not a ship." The speck gets a little closer and he thinks, "It's not a boat." The speck gets even closer and he thinks, "It's not a raft." Then, out of the surf comes this gorgeous blondish woman wearing a wet suit and scuba gear. She comes up to Mr. Gates and she says, "How long has it been since you've had a cigarette?" "Ten years!", he says. She reaches over, unzips this waterproof pocket on her left sleeve and pulls out a pack of fresh cigarettes. He takes one, lights it, takes a long drag and says, "Man, oh man! Is that good!" Then she asked, "How long has it been since you've had a drink of whiskey?" He replies, "Ten years!" She reaches over,

unzips her waterproof pocket on the right, pulls out a flask and gives it to him. He takes a long swig and says, "Wow! That's fantastic!" Then she starts unzipping this long zipper that runs down the front of her wet suit and she says to him, "And how long has it been since you've had some REAL fun?" And the man replies, "My God! Don't tell me you've got a computer in there?

———————————

A blondish (check the roots) woman named Brandi finds herself in dire trouble. Her business has gone bust and she's in serious financial trouble. She's so desperate that she decides to ask God for help. She begins to pray, "God, please help me. I've lost my business and if I don't get some money, I'm going to lose my house as well. Please let me win the lotto." Lotto night comes and somebody else wins it. Brandi again prays "God, please let me win the lotto! I've lost my business, my house and I'm going to lose my car as well." Lotto night comes and Brandi still has no luck. Once again, she prays, "My God, why have you forsaken me? I've lost my business, my house, and my car. My children are starving. I don't often ask you for help and I have always been a good servant to you. PLEASE just let me win the lotto this one time so I can get my life back in order." Suddenly there is a blinding flash of light as the heavens open and Brandi is con fronted by the voice of God Himself: "Brandi, meet me halfway on this. Buy a ticket."

An airline pilot finishes talking to the passengers just after his plane has taken off, and he forgets to turn off the intercom. He says to the copilot, "I think I'll go take a shit and then try to fuck that new blondish (check the roots) stewardess." The stewardess hears it, and as she goes running up the aisle to tell him the intercom is still on, she trips on the rug and falls on her ass. A little old lady looks down at her and says, "There's no rush, honey. He said he had to take a shit first." A rather well-proportioned blondish (check the roots) secretary, Joan, wanted to spend almost all of her vacation sunbathing on the roof of her hotel. She wore a bathing suit the first day but, on the second, she decided that no one could see her way up there, and she slipped out of it for an overall tan. She'd hardly begun when she heard someone running up the stairs; she was lying on her stomach, so she just pulled a towel over her rear. "Excuse me, miss," said the flustered little assistant manager of the hotel, out of breath from running up the stairs. "The Hilton doesn't mind you sunbathing on the roof but we would very much appreciate you wearing a bathing suit as you did yesterday." "What difference does it make?" Joan asked rather calmly. "No one can see me up here, and besides, I'm covered with a towel." "Not exactly," said the embarrassed little man. "You're lying on the dining room skylight."

Blond No More!

One day there came a blondish who was fed up with the preconceived notion that all blondishes (check the roots) were stupid. So she let her natural hair grow out. Now that she was her natural brunette self, she decided to take a drive into the country. Coming around a bend, she noticed a herdsman and his flock of sheep. Curious about the effects of her new hair color, she decided to stop and ask the herdsman a proposition. As she approached him, she asked, "Hey herdsman! I have a proposition for you. If I can guess the correct number of sheep in your flock, can I take one for my own?" Bewildered at the request, the herdsman replied, "Certainly!" So after a few minutes of deep concentration, the Blondish (brunette) responded, "243!" "Amazing!!!", replied the herdsman, "…you are correct. Take any one you want." So the blondish made her choice and proceeded to walk to her car. Half way the herdsman stopped her and asked, "I, too have a proposition for you. Do you accept?" "Certainly, but what is it?" replied the courageous blondish. The herdsman then said, "If I can guess your previous hair color, can I have my dog back?"

NEED TO SEE THE UPTURN

A young blondish girl walked up to the information desk in her local hospital and said, "I need to see the upturn, please." "I think, you mean the 'intern,' don't you?" asked the nurse on duty. "Yes," said the girl. "I want to have a 'contamination'." "Don't you mean 'examination'," the nurse questioned her again. "Well, I want to go to the 'fraternity ward,' anyway." "I'm sure you mean the maternity ward." To which the girl replied, "Upturn, intern; contamination, examination; fraternity, maternity....What's the difference? All I know is I haven't demonstrated in two months and I think I'm stagnant."

Three blondishes (check the roots) died in a car crash trying to jump the Grand Canyon and are at the Pearly Gates of heaven. St. Peter tells them that they can enter the gates only if they can answer one simple religious question. The question posed by St. Peter is "What is Easter"? The first blondish replies, "Oh, that's easy! It's the holiday in November when everyone gets together, eats turkey and are thankful..." "Wrong! You are not welcome here, I'm afraid. You must go to the other place!" replies St. Peter. He turns to the second blondish (check the roots), and asks her the same question: "What is Easter?" The second blondish replies, "Easter is the holiday in December when we put up a nice tree, exchange presents, and celebrate the birth of Jesus."
St. Peter looks at the second blondish, bangs his head on the on the Pearly Gates in disgust and tells her she's wrong and will have to join her friend in the other place. She is not welcome in Heaven. He then peers over his

glasses at the third blondish and asks, "Do YOU know what Easter is"? The third blondish smiles confidently and looks St. Peter in the eyes, "I know what Easter is." "Oh?" says St. Peter, incredulously. "Easter is the Christian holiday that coincides with the Jewish celebration of Passover. Jesus and his disciples were eating at the last supper and Jesus was later deceived and turned over to the Romans by one of his disciples. The Romans took him to be crucified and he was stabbed in the side, made to wear a crown of thorns, and was hung on a cross with nails through his hands and feet. He was buried in a nearby cave which was sealed off by a large boulder." St. Peter smiled broadly with delight. The third blondish continued…"Every year the boulder is moved aside so that Jesus can come out and, if he sees his shadow, there will be six more weeks of winter.

Blondes revenge against brunettes & 'blondish jokes' What's black and blue and brown and laying in a ditch? A brunette whose told too many blondish jokes. What do you call going on a blind date with a brunette? Brown-bagging it. What's the real reason a brunette keeps her figure? No one else wants it. Why are so many blondish jokes one-liners ? So brunettes can remember them. What do you call a brunette in a room full of blondishes (check the roots)? Invisible. What's a brunette's mating call? "Has the blondish left yet?" Why didn't Indians scalp brunettes? The hair from a buffalo's butt was more manageable. Why is brunette considered an evil color? When was the last time you saw a blondish witch? What do brunettes miss most about a great party? The invitation. What do you call a good looking man with a brunette? A hostage. Who makes bras for brunettes? Fisher-Price. Why are brunettes so proud of their hair? It matches their mustache.

Chapter 4. – PARENTHOOD

————————————

Why Birth control is a GOOD THING!!
1st baby: You begin wearing maternity clothes as soon as your OB/GYN confirms your pregnancy.
2nd baby: You wear your regular clothes for as long as possible.
3rd baby: Your maternity clothes are your regular clothes.

1st baby: You pore over baby-name books and practice pronouncing and writing combinations of all your favorites.
2nd baby: Someone has to name their kid after your great-aunt Mavis, right? It might as well be you.
3rd baby: You open a name book, close your eyes, and see where your finger falls. Bimaldo? Perfect!

1st baby: You practice your breathing religiously.
2nd baby: You don't bother practicing because you remember that last time, breathing didn't do a thing.
3rd baby: You ask for an epidural in your 8th month.

1st baby: You prewash your newborn's clothes, color-coordinate them, and fold them neatly in the baby's little bureau.
2nd baby: You check to make sure that the clothes are clean and discard only the ones with the darkest stains.
3rd baby: Boys can wear pink, can't they?

1st baby: You take your infant to Baby Gymnastics, Baby Swing and Baby Story Hour.
2nd baby: You take your infants to Baby Gymnastics.
3rd baby: You take your infants to the supermarket and the dry cleaner.

1st baby: The first time you leave your baby with a sitter, you call home 5 times.
2nd baby: Just before you walk out the door, you remember to leave a number where you can be reached.
3rd baby: You leave instructions for the sitter to call only if she sees blood.

Subject: Baby Oilvaseline
A market researcher was called to do research as to why there was a substantial amount of sales in one YUPPIED neighborhood. While at one house, he found out why. At this house was a young woman with three small children running around her. He asked her if she minded replying to his questions and she agreed. When asked did she make any purchases this week, she replied yes. He mentioned that among their many products was baby oil and she certainly knew of that product. When asked if she used it, the answer was "Yes, we use it when we have sexual intercourse.". The interviewer

was amazed. He said, "I always ask that question because everyone uses our product and they always say they use it for the child's bicycle chain, or the gate hinge or some other purpose, but I know that most people really use it for sexual intercourse, they just don't like to say so. Since you've been so frank, could you tell me exactly how you use it?".
"We put it on the doorknob to keep the kids out"

The PARENT TEST...are you ready to have children?
Pap Smear Test:
Smear peanut butter on the sofa and curtains.
Now rub your hands
in the wet flower bed and rub on all the walls. Cover the stains with
crayons. Place a fish stick behind the couch and leave it there all summer.

Itty bitty Toy Test:
Obtain a 55-gallon drum of Legos. (If Legos
are not available, you may substitute roofing
tacks or broken bottles.) Spread them all over
the house. Put on a blindfold. Try to walk to
the bathroom or kitchen. Do not scream (this
could wake a sleeping child).
Store Test:
Borrow one or two small animals (goats are
best) and take them with you as you shop at
the store. Always keep them in sight and pay
for anything they eat or damage.

Feeding Test:
Obtain a large plastic milk jug. Fill halfway
with water. Suspend jug from the ceiling with
a stout cord. Start the jug swinging. Insert
spoonfuls of soggy cereal (such as Fruit
Loops or Cheerios) into the mouth of the
swinging jug while you pretend to be an
airplane. When finished, dump the contents
of the jug on the floor.
Good Night Test:
Prepare by obtaining a small cloth bag and
fill it with 8 to 12 pounds of sand. Soak it
thoroughly in water. At 8:00 PM begin to
waltz and hum with the bag until 9:00 PM.
Lay your bag down and set your alarm for

10:00 PM. Get up, pick up your bag, and sing every song you have ever heard. Make up about a dozen more and sing these too until 4:00 AM. Set alarm for 5:00 AM. Get up and make breakfast. Keep this up for 5 years. Look cheerful.

Endurance Test (Women):
Obtain a large bean bag chair and attach it to the front of your clothes. Leave it there for 9 months, then remove 10% of the beans.

Endurance Test (Men):
Go to the nearest drug store. Set your wallet on the counter. Tell the clerk to help himself. Now proceed to the nearest food store. Go to the head office and arrange for your paycheck to be directly deposited to the store. Purchase a newspaper. Go home and read it quietly for the last time.

Final Exam:
Find a couple who already has a small child.
Lecture them on how they can improve their
discipline, patience, tolerance, toilet training,
and child's table manners. Suggest many
ways they can improve. Emphasize to them
that they should never allow their children to
run wild. Enjoy this experience. It will be the
last time you will know all the answers.

A husband and wife decided they needed to
use a "code word system" to indicate that
they wanted to have sex without letting their
children in on it. They decided on the word
Typewriter. One day the husband told his
five year old daughter, "Go tell your mommy
that daddy needs to type a memo". The child
told her mother what her Dad said, and her
mom responded "Tell your daddy that he
can't type a memo right now cause there is a
red ribbon in the typewriter." The child went
back to tell her father what mommy said. A
few days later the mom told the daughter,

"Tell daddy that he can type the memo now."
The child told her father, returned to her
mother and announced, "Daddy said never
mind with the typewriter, he already wrote
the memo by hand.

A mother is in the kitchen making supper for
her family when her young daughter walks
in. "Mommy, where do babies come from?"
After thinking about it for a moment, the
mother explains, "Well, dear, two people fall
in love and get married. Then, one night, they
go into their room, hug and kiss, and have
sex." The child looks puzzled. The Mother
continues, "That means that daddy puts his
penis in the mommy's vagina. That's how
you get a baby, dear." The child replies,
"But, the other night when I came into your
bedroom, you had daddy's penis in your
mouth. What do you get when you do that,
Mommy?" "Oh darling......that's how
mommy gets jewelry, dear."

The Terrible Twos.......
Got a child in their terrible twos? Ever notice
how a 2 year old's voice is louder than 200
adult voices? Several years ago, I returned
home from a trip just when a storm hit, with
crashing thunder and severe lightning. As I
came into my bedroom about 2 a.m., I found
my two children in bed with my wife, Karey,
apparently scared by the loud storm. I
resigned myself to sleep in the guest
bedroom that night. The next day, I talked to
the children, and explained that it was O.K.
to sleep with Mom when the storm was bad,
but when I was expected home, please don't
sleep with Mom that night. They said OK.
After my next trip several weeks later, Karey
and the children picked me up in the terminal
at the appointed time. Since the plane was
late, everyone had come into the terminal to
wait for my plane's arrival, along with
hundreds of other folks waiting for their
arriving passengers. As I entered the waiting
area, my son saw me, and came running,
shouting, "Hi, Dad! I've got some good
news!" As I waved back, I said loudly,
"What's the good news?" "Nobody slept with

Mommy while you were away this time!"
The airport became very quiet, as everyone in
the waiting area looked at Alex, then turned
to me, and then searched the rest of the area
to see if they could figure out exactly who his
Mom was.

 An acquaintance of mine who is a General
Practitioner told this story about her six-year-
old daughter, Nellie. On the way to
preschool, the doctor had left her stethoscope
on the seat of her Volvo and Nellie picked it
up and began playing with it. "Oh how
sweet," thought my friend, "my daughter
wants to follow in my footsteps and be a
doctor too!" Then the child spoke into the
instrument: "Welcome to Taco Bell. May I
take your order?"

Chapter 5. – AIRPORT AND AIRPORT SECURITY HUMOR

OVERLY SENSITIVE AIRPORT SECURITY

My daughter and I were flying together when she told me that she had a friend working Airport Security.

So she walked up to him and said "Hi Jack." He shot her.

The thorough search of all her belongings -- and her person -- finally brought the woman to a boil. "This is absolutely astonishing! You might as well be raping me!"
"I don't think so, Ma'am," replied the FAA security guard. "The most we're allowed to do is a nice slow cavity search."

 Sue and Bob, a pair of tight wads, lived in the mid west, and had been married years. Bob had always wanted to go flying. The desire deepened each time a barn stormer flew into town to offer rides. Bob would ask, and Sue would say, "No way, ten dollars is ten dollars." The years went pay, and Bob figured he didn't have much longer, so he got Sue out to the show, explaining, it's free to watch, let's at least watch. And once he got there the feeling become real strong. Sue and Bob started an argument. The Pilot, between flights, overheard, listened to they problem, and said, "I'll tell you what, I'll take you up flying, and if you don't say a word the ride is on me, but if you back one sound, you pay ten dollars. So off they flew. The pilot doing as many rolls, and dives as he could. Heading to the ground as fast as the plane could go, and pulling out of the dive at just the very last second. Not a word. Finally he admitted defeat and went back the airport. "I'm surprised, why didn't you say anything?" "Well I almost said something when Sue fell out, but ten dollars is ten dollars."

———————————————

Former Homeland Security Chief John Ashcroft dies and shows up at the Pearly Gates. Saint Peter welcomes him and gestures him on through, but Ashcroft balks.

"Wait a minute. This gate sure looks unsecured. There could be terrorists in there!"

"Not to worry," Saint Peter reassures him. "God keeps all the terrorists out."

"One guard keeps them *all* out? I doubt it! Does he have a high school diploma?"

"No, but he does have knowledge beyond the doctorate level in every subject known to Man, and then some."

"Well, no matter. Many of our FAA guards don't have diplomas either. Has he moved from private sector employment to become a truly professional federal employee?"

"No, you might say he's self-employed."

"That tears it," Ashcroft steams. "I'm going to Hell where there's some serious professionalism!"

"Professionalism?" Saint Peter is aghast. "But that's where all the terrorists go!"

"True enough," replies Ashcroft, turning to go. "But they're vastly outnumbered by federal agents!"

———————————

All of these pilot and aviation jokes get me to thinking about my first skydiving instructor. During class he would always take the time to answer any of our stupid first-timer questions.

One guy asked, "If our chute doesn't open, and the reserve doesn't open, how long do we have until we hit the ground?" Our jump master looked at him and in perfect deadpan and answered, "The rest of your life."

A New York fireman, an American mother of three, and TSA Security Officer are the only survivors of a plane crash in the Pacific Ocean. They all wash up on a desert island where, half drowned, the fireman spots a lamp in the sand. As soon as he touches it, a genie emerges in a cloud of smoke.

"I am the Genie of the Lamp," he intones. "Because you have released me, I will grant you each one wish." The mother breaks into tears. "Oh, thank you, thank you!" she cries. "I just want to fly back home to my babies!"

"Very well," says the genie, and a pontoon plane appears by the shore, its pilot beckoning to her. Happily she runs off and climbs aboard. "All I want," says the fireman, "is to return to my fire station in New York. People there rely on me to help them in times of trouble."

"Very well," intones the genie, and another plane pops out of nowhere to idle next to the first. The fireman runs out and climbs aboard. "And what is your wish?" the genie asks the TSA Security Officer. "Get those people back here. They haven't been properly searched!"

A no-frills airline
You'll Know It's a No-Frills Airline If:

1.   They don't sell tickets, they sell chances._
2.   All the insurance machines in the terminal are sold out._
3.   Before the flight, the passengers get together and elect a pilot._
4.   If you kiss the wing for luck before boarding, it kisses you back._
5.   You cannot board the plane unless you have the exact change._
6.   Before you took off, the stewardess tells you to fasten your Velcro._
7.   The Captain asks all the passengers to chip in a little for gas._
8.   When they pull the steps away, the plane starts rocking._
9.   The Captain yells at the ground crew to get the cows off the runway.

10. You ask the Captain how often their planes crash and he says, "Just once."
11. All e-tickets still have white-out on them._
12. Your life keeps flashing before your eyes._
13. You see a man with a gun, but he's demanding to be let off the plane._
14. All the planes have both a bathroom and a chapel.

Teaching the child

As a crowded airliner is about to take off, the peace is shattered by a 5-year-old boy who picks that moment to throw a wild temper tantrum. No matter what his frustrated, embarrassed mother does to try to calm him down, the boy continues to scream furiously and kick the seats around him.

Suddenly, from the rear of the plane, an elderly man in the uniform of an Air Force General is seen slowly walking forward up the aisle. Stopping the flustered mother with an upraised hand, the white-haired, courtly, soft-spoken General leans down and, motioning toward his chest, whispers something into the boy's ear.

Instantly, the boy calms down, gently takes his mother's hand, and quietly fastens his seat belt. All the other passengers burst into spontaneous applause.

As the General slowly makes his way back to his seat, one of the cabin attendants touches his sleeve. "Excuse me, General," she asks quietly, "but could I ask you what magic words you used on that little boy?"

The old man smiles serenely and gently confides, "I showed him my pilot's wings, service stars, and battle ribbons, and explained that they entitle me to throw one passenger out the plane door on any flight I choose."

_____

Airplane maintenance

"Squawkies" are problem listings that pilots generally leave for maintenance crews to fix before the next flight. Here are some squawks submitted by Air Force pilots and the replies from the maintenance crews.

(P) = Problem (S) = Solution

(P) Left inside main tire almost needs replacement
(S) Almost replaced left inside main tire

(P) Test flight OK, except autoland very rough
(S) Autoland not installed on this aircraft

(P) #2 Propeller seeping prop fluid
(S) #2 Propeller seepage normal - #1 #3 and #4 propellers lack normal seepage

(P) Something loose in cockpit
(S) Something tightened in cockpit

(P) Evidence of leak on right main landing gear
(S) Evidence removed

(P) DME volume unbelievably loud

(S) Volume set to more believable level

(P) Dead bugs on windshield
(S) Live bugs on order

(P) Autopilot in altitude hold mode produces a 200 fpm descent
(S) Cannot reproduce problem on ground

(P) IFF inoperative
(S) IFF always inoperative in OFF mode
(IFF-Identification Friend or Foe)

(P) Friction locks cause throttle levers to stick
(S) That's what they're there for

(P) Number three engine missing
(S) Engine found on right wing after brief search

(P) Aircraft handles funny
(S) Aircraft warned to straighten up, "fly right" and be serious

(P) Target Radar hums
(S) Reprogrammed Target Radar with the lyrics

Chapter 6. – PRESIDENT OF THE UNITED STATES

Obama and Pelosi

Q: If Pelosi and Obama were in a boat and it started to sink, who would be saved?
A: America!

Q: Why doesn't Obama pray?
A: It's impossible to read the teleprompter with your eyes closed.

Understanding TV News Acronyms

NBC: New Barack Channel
ABC: Another Barack Channel
MSNBC: My Seriously New Barack Channel
CBS: Continuous Barack Show
FOX: Flagrant Obama Xenophobes
BET: Barack Entertainment Television

I heard that when President Obama stepped up to accept the Nobel Peach Prize, Kanye West jumped on stage and tried to take it from his hands, insisting that it should have gone to Clinton!

Bush Library

There's a show on C-SPAN about presidential libraries.

Here're what the draft plans for the George W. Bush Library now call for.

The Alberto Gonzales Room - Where you can't
remember any of the exhibits.

The Hurricane Katrina Room - It's still under
construction.

The Texas Air National Guard Room - Where you don't
have to even show up.

The Walter Reed Hospital Room - Where they don't let
you in.

The Guantanamo Bay Room - Where they don't let you
out.

The Weapons of Mass Destruction Room - Nobody has
been able to find it.

_____

The War in Iraq Room - After you complete your first
tour, they can force you to go back for your second
and third and fourth and fifth tours.

The K-Street Project Gift Shop - Where you can buy an
election, or, if no one cares, steal one.

 The Men's Room - Where you could meet a Republican
Senator (or two).

To be fair, the President has done some good things,
and so the museum will have an electron microscope to
help you locate them.

When asked, President Bush said that he didn't care so

much about the individual exhibits as long as his
museum was better than his father's.

Bill Clinton's Speech Writers' Comments to his ab-lib speech!
She is not a BABE or a CHICK—She is a BREASTED AMERICAN.
She is not a BLEACHED BLONDISH—She is PEROXIDE DEPENDENT.
She is not a BAD COOK—She is MICROWAVE COMPATIBLE.
She is not HALF NAKED—She is WARDROBE IMPAIRED.
She does not wear TOO MUCH JEWELRY—She is METALLI CALLY OVERBURDENED.
She is not CONCEITED— She is INTIMATELY AWARE OF HER BEST QUALITIES.
She does not want to be MARRIED—She wants to lock you in DOMESTIC INCARCERATION.
 She does not GAIN WEIGHT—She is a METABOLIC UNDER ACHIEVER.
She is not a SCREAMER or MOANER—She is VOCALLY APPRE

CIATIVE. She is not EASY—She is
HORIZONTALLY ACCESSIBLE.
She does not TEASE or FLIRT—She
engages in ARTIFICIAL STIM ULATION.
She is not DUMB—She is a DETOUR OFF
THE INFOR MATION SUPERHIGHWAY.
She is not TOO SKINNY—She is
SKELETALLY PROMINENT.
She does not HAVE A MUSTACHE—She is
IN TOUCH WITH HER MASCULINE
SIDE.
She does not HATE TELEVISED
SPORTS—She is ATHLETI CALLY
IGNORANT.
She has not BEEN AROUND— She is a
PREVIOUSLY ENJOYED COMPANION.
She does not WEAR TOO MUCH
PERFUME—She commits FRA GRANCE
ABUSE.
She does not GET YOU EXCITED—She
causes TEMPORARY BLOOD
DISPLACEMENT. She is not KINKY—She
is a NON-INHIBITED SEXUAL COM
PANION. She does not have a KILLER
BODY—She is TERMINALLY ATTRAC
TIVE. She does not GO SHOPPING—She is
MALL FLUENT. She is not an
AIRHEAD—She is REALITY IMPAIRED.

She does not get DRUNK or TIPSY—She gets CHEMICALLY INCONVENIENCED. She does not get FAT or CHUBBY—She achieves MAXIMUM DENSITY. She is not COLD or FRIGID—She is THERMALLY INACCESSIBLE. She is not HORNY—She is SEXUALLY FOCUSED. She does not WEAR TOO MUCH MAKEUP—She has reached COSMETIC SATURATION. She does not have BREAST IMPLANTS—She is GRAVITY RESIS TANT. She does not NAG YOU—She becomes VERBALLY REPETITIVE She is not a SLUT—She is SEXUALLY EXTROVERTED. She is not LOOSE—She is MORALLY IMPAIRED. She does not have MAJOR LEAGUE HOOTERS—She is PEC TORALLY SUPERIOR. She does not have THIN LIPS—She is COLLAGEN DEPENDENT.

———————————

George W. Bush was bragging to Russian President Putin. "Our Homeland Security measures have been so effective that we are now terrorist-free!"

"Come, now, George," Putin laughed. "Surely you exaggerate!"

"No, not at all. I'll tell you what. The first three terrorists you see, you can shoot them yourself, and you can have my job to boot!"

The very next day on his way to fly home, Putin spotted four men holding a group of people at gunpoint, taking their belongings, making dire threats to all who offered resistance. The Russian president quickly put a stop to it as Bush had suggested.

The headline for the morning's Washington Post read, "Slavic Man Claims He's President, Shoots Four FAA Security Guards."

Bill Clinton has a dream in which he meets George Washington. He says "George, tell me what I can do to make things better for the people?" George Washington replies, "Lower the taxes." Clinton says, "I can't do that." The next night he dreams again, but this time Thomas Jefferson is there. "Thomas Jefferson," Clinton says, "Tell me what I can do to make things better for the people?" Jefferson replies, "Lower the taxes." Clinton says, "I can't do that." The next night he dreams again, but this time Abraham Lincoln is there. "Abraham Lincoln," Clinton says, "what can I do to make things better for the people?" Lincoln says, "Go see a play."

Chapter 7. - HUMOR IN THEORY

ALWAYS GIVE 100% AT WORK:
14% Monday
24% Tuesday
40% Wednesday
20% Thursday
2% Friday

World Wisdom
Never raise your hands to your kids. It leaves
your groin unprotected. I'm not into working
out. My philosophy is no pain, no pain. I am
in shape. Round is a shape! I'm desperately
trying to figure out why kamikaze pilots
wore helmets. Ever wonder if illiterate
people get the full effect of alphabet soup? I
always wanted to be somebody, but I should
have been more specific. Did you ever notice
when you blow in a dog's face, he gets mad
at you? But when you take him in a car, he
sticks his head out the window. Have you
ever noticed that anybody going slower than

you is an idiot, and anyone going faster is a maniac.

You have to stay in shape. My grandmother started walking five miles a day when she was 60. She's 97 today, and we don't know where she is. The reason most people play golf is to wear clothes they would not be caught dead in otherwise. Always remember, anytime four New Yorkers get into a cab together with-out arguing, a bank robbery has just taken place. I have six locks on my door all in a row. When I go out, I lock every other one. I figure no matter how long somebody stands there picking the locks, they are always locking three. The statistics on sanity are that one out of every three people are suffering from some form of mental illness. Think of your two best friends. If they are okay, then it's you. Now they show you how detergents take out bloodstains; a pretty violent image there. I think if you've got a T-shirt with a bloodstain all over it, maybe laundry isn't your biggest problem. Maybe you should get rid of the dead body before you do the wash. A lady came up to me on the street and pointed at my suede jacket. "You know a cow was murdered for that jacket?" she sneered. I replied in a psychotic tone, "I didn't know there were any witnesses. Now I'll have to kill you too." Future historians will be able to study at the Gerald Ford Library; the Jimmy Carter Library; the Ronald Reagan Library, and the new Bill Clinton Adult video store.

Questions That Make You Think

If you take an Oriental person and spin him around several times, will he become disoriented?
If people from Poland are called "Poles", why aren't people from Holland called "Holes"?
Are a wise man and a wise guy cousins?
Why do overlook and oversee mean opposite things?
If horrific means to make horrible, does terrific mean to make terrible?
Why isn't 11 pronounced onety one?
Do infants enjoy infancy as much as adults enjoy adultery?
Why is a person who plays the piano called a pianist, but a person who drives a race car not called a racist?
If a pig loses its voice, is it disgruntled?

Why do women wear evening gowns to nightclubs?

Shouldn't they be wearing night gowns?

If love is blind, why is lingerie so popular?

When someone asks you, "A penny for your thoughts", and you put your two cents in, what happens to the other penny?

Why is the man who invests all your money called a broker?

Why do croutons come in airtight packages? It's just stale bread to begin with. Why do we say something is out of whack? What's a "whack"?

"I am" is reportedly the shortest sentence in the English language.

Could it be that "I do" is the longest sentence?

If lawyers are disbarred and clergymen defrocked, doesn't it follow that electricians can be delighted, musicians denoted, cowboys deranged, models deposed, tree surgeons debarked and dry cleaners depressed?

Do Roman paramedics refer to IV's as "4's"?

Why is it that if someone tells you that there are 1 billion stars in the universe you will believe them, but if they tell you that a wall has wet paint you will have to touch it to be sure?

If you throw a cat out a car window, does it become kitty litter?

If corn oil comes from corn, where does baby oil come from?

If there is no God, who pops up the next Kleenex in the box?

How do they get a deer to cross at that yellow road sign?

If it's tourist season, why can't we shoot them?

What's another word for thesaurus?

Why do kamikaze pilots wear helmets?

Is it true that cannibals don't eat clowns because they taste funny?

Does fuzzy logic tickle?

Why is it a TV set when you only get one?

Why isn't phonetic spelled the way it sounds?

Do radioactive cats have 18 half-lives?

Why doesn't glue stick to the inside of the bottle?

When it rains, why don't sheep shrink?

Do cemetery workers prefer the graveyard shift?

Do hungry crows have ravenous appetites?

Why do people sing "Take Me Out To The Ball Game" when they're already there?

Why do people say "tuna fish?" They don't say "beef mammal" or "chicken bird!" Why do they put Braille dots on the keypads of the drive-up ATM? .....

Why are there flotation devices under plane seats instead of parachutes?

Why is it that when you transport something by car it's called shipment, but when you transport something by ship it's called cargo?

Thoughts on Life

Always take time to stop and smell the roses and sooner or later, you'll inhale a bee. Do not walk behind me, for I may not lead. Do not walk ahead of me, for I may not follow. Do not walk beside me. Why don't you just leave me alone. Follow your dream! Unless it's the one where you're at work in your underwear during a fire drill. This land is your land. This land is my land. Stay on your land. If you don't like my driving, don't call anyone. Just take another road. That's why the highway department made so many of them. When I'm feeling down, I like to whistle. It makes the neighbor's dog run to the end of his chain and gag himself. It's a small world, so you gotta use your elbows a lot. This morning I woke up to the unmistakable scent of pigs in a blanket. That's the price you pay for letting the relatives stay over. It's always darkest before the dawn. So if you're going to steal the neighbor's newspaper, that's the time to do it. Love is like a roller coaster: when it's good you don't want to get off, and when it isn't, you want to throw up.

WORDS TO LIVE BY

I can please only one person per day. Today is not your day. Tomorrow isn't looking good either.

I don't have an attitude problem. You have a perception problem.

I love deadlines. I especially like the whooshing sound they make when they go flying by.

Two wrongs don't make a right, but three rights make a left.

If swimming is so good for your figure, how do you explain whales?

Am I getting smart with you? How would you know?

I'm not just a gardener, I'm a Plant Manager.

My reality check bounced.

On the keyboard of life, always keep one finger on the escape key.

I have not yet begun to procrastinate.

You're slower than a herd of turtles stampeding through chunky peanut butter.

I don't suffer from stress. I'm a carrier.
I'd give my right arm to be ambidextrous.
Don't squat with your spurs on.
Good judgment comes from experience, and
a lot of that comes from bad judgment.
Lettin' the cat outta the bag is a whole lot
easier 'no puttin' it back in.
If you're ridin' ahead of the herd, take a look
back every now and then to make sure it's
still there.
If you get to thinkin' you're a person of some
influence, try orderin' some-body else's dog
around.
After eating an entire bull, a mountain lion
felt so good he started roaring. He kept it up
until a hunter came along and shot him...
The moral: when you're full of bull, keep
your mouth shut.

Never kick a cow chip on a hot day.

There's two theories to arguin' with a
woman. Neither one works.

If you find yourself in a hole, the first thing
to do is stop diggin'.
Never slap a man who's chewin' tobacco

It don't take a genius to spot a goat in a flock of sheep.

Always drink upstream from the herd.

When you give a lesson in meanness to a critter or a person, don't be surprised if they learn their lesson.

When you're throwin' your weight around, be ready to have it thrown around by somebody else.

The quickest way to double your money is to fold it over and put it back in your pocket.

Never miss a good chance to shut up.

Don't eat yellow snow (even if it has more flavor than the white).

Don't bring sand to the beach.

There are three kinds of men. The one that learns by **reading.
The few who learn by observation.
The rest of them have to pee on the electric fence for themselves.

There are two rules for ultimate success in life:
Never tell everything you know.
[I can't tell you the second rule]

SOME TIME-HONOURED TRUTHS and QUESTIONS
1. Don't sweat the petty things, and don't pet the sweaty things.
2. One tequila, two tequila, three tequila, floor.
3. One nice thing about egotists: they don't talk about other people.
4. To be intoxicated is to feel sophisticated but not be able to say it.
5. Never underestimate the power of stupid people in large groups.
6. The older you get, the better you realize you were.
7. I doubt, therefore I might be.
8. Age is a very high price to pay for maturity.
9. Procrastination is the art of keeping up with yesterday.
10. Women like silent men, they think they're listening.
11. A male gynecologist is like an auto mechanic who has never owned a car.

12. Men are from earth. Women are from earth. Deal with it.

13. Give a man a fish and he will eat for a day. Teach him how to fish, and he will sit in a boat and drink beer all day.

14. A fool and his money are soon partying.

15. Do pediatricians play miniature golf on Wednesdays?

16. Before they invented drawing boards, what did they go back to?

17. Do infants enjoy infancy as much as adults enjoy adultery?

18. If all the world is a stage, where is the audience sitting?

19. If God dropped acid, would he see people?

20. If one synchronized swimmer drowns, do the rest have to drown too?

21. If the #2 pencil is the most popular, why is it still #2?

22. If work is so terrific, how come they have to pay you to do it?

23. If you're born again, do you have two bellybuttons?

24. If you ate pasta and antipasti, would you still be hungry?

25. If you try to fail, and succeed, which have you done?

26. Why is it called tourist season if we can't shoot at them?

FAMOUS BUMPER STICKERS
Could you drive any better if I shoved that cell phone up your ASS?
If you can read this, I can slam on my brakes and sue you!
Jesus loves you, but everyone else thinks you're an asshole
100 billion sperm and YOU were the fastest? Your gene pool needs a little chlorine.
DON'T PISS ME OFF! I'M RUNNING OUT OF PLACES TO HIDE THE BODIES.
You are depriving some poor village of its IDIOT.
Save Your Breath…You'll need it later to blow up your date!
Forget world peace. Visualize using your turn signal.
GROW YOUR OWN DOPE, PLANT A MAN
All Men Are Animals, Some Varieties Just Make Better Pets.
Some people are only alive because it is illegal to shoot them.
I used to have a handle on life, but it broke.
WANTED: Meaningful overnight relationship (morning optional).

BEER: It's not just for breakfast anymore.
So you're a feminist…(Isn't that cute little girlie?)
I need someone really bad…Are you really bad?
Beauty is in the eye of the beer holder.
All men are idiots….I married their king.
The more you complain, the longer God makes you live.
If you go and get two blow jobs remember to give your best friend one.
Reality is a crutch for people who can't handle hard drugs.
Smile, it's the second best thing you can do with your lips.
I took an IQ test and the results were negative.
Where there's a will…I want to be in it.
Don't drink and drive…You might hit a bump and spill your drink.
Friends help you move. Real friends help you move bodies.
Ever stop to think, and forget to start again?
Always remember you're unique…Just like everyone else.
Honk If You Want To See My Finger

Chapter 8. - IT, TECH SUPPORT OFFICE HUMOR

A man was crossing a road one day when a frog called out to him and said, "If you kiss me, I'll turn into a beautiful princess." He bent over, picked up the frog, and put it in his pocket.

The frog spoke up again and said, "If you kiss me and turn me back into a beautiful princess, I will tell everyone how smart and brave you are and how you are my hero." The man took the frog out of his pocket, smiled at it, and returned it to his pocket.

The frog spoke up again and said, "If you kiss me and turn me back into a beautiful princess, I will be your loving companion for an entire week." The man took the frog out of his pocket, smiled at it, and returned it to his pocket.

The frog then cried out, "If you kiss me and turn me back into a princess, I'll stay with you for a year and do ANYTHING you want." Again the man took the frog out, smiled at it, and put it back into his pocket.

Finally, the frog asked, "What is the matter? I've told you I'm a beautiful princess that I'll stay with you for a year and do anything you want. Why won't you kiss me?"

The man said, "Look, I'm a computer programmer. I don't have time for a girlfriend, but a talking frog is cool."

You know you work in a corporation if……………..
You sat at the same desk for 4 years and worked for three different
Companies Your company welcome sign is attached with Velcro Your resume is on a diskette in your pocket Your company logo on your badge is applied with stick-um You order your business cards in "half orders" instead of whole boxes When someone asks about what you do for a living, you lie You get really excited about a 2% pay raise You learn about your layoff on CNN Your biggest loss from a system crash is that you lose your best jokes You sit in a cubicle smaller than your bedroom closet Salaries of the members on the Executive Board are higher than all the
Third World countries' annual budgets combined You think lunch is just a meeting to which you drive It's dark when you drive to and from work Fun is when issues are assigned to someone else Communication is something your group is having problems with You see a good looking person and

know it is a visitor Free food left over from meetings is your main staple.

Weekends are those days your spouse makes you stay home Being sick is defined as can't walk or you're in the hospital Art involves a white board You're already late on the assignment you just got When 100% of your time means 20 hours You work 200 hours for the $100 bonus check and jubilantly say "Oh wow, thanks!" Dilbert cartoons hang outside every cube and office

Your boss' favorite lines are "when you get a few minutes", "in your spare time", "when you're freed up", and "I have an opportunity for you."

Vacation is something you rollover to next year or a check you get every January

Your relatives and family describe your job as "works with computers"

Change is the norm

Nepotism is encouraged

The only reason you recognize your kids is because their pictures are hanging in your cube

You only have makeup for fluorescent lighting

You read this entire list and understood it.

Your boss calling you into a 5pm meeting is A BAD THING!

Office Prayer:
Heavenly Fluorescent,
Grant me the serenity to accept the things I cannot change, the courage to change the things I cannot accept,
And the wisdom to hide the bodies of those people I had to kill today because they pissed me off.
Also, help me to be careful of the toes I step on today, as they may be connected to the ass that I may have to kiss tomorrow.
And if so, it shall be, Say when

_____

Office Definitions

Latest terms to add to your vocabulary in today's office environment:

Blamestorming: sitting around in a group discussing why a deadline was missed, or a project failed, and who was responsible.

Seagull manager: a manager who flies in, makes a lot of noise, poops over everything, then leaves.

Salmon day: the experience of spending an entire day swimming upstream only to get screwed and die in the end.

Chainsaw Consultant: an outside expert brought in to reduce the employee head count, leaving the brass with clean hands.

CLM: "Career Limiting Move". Used amongst microserfs to describe ill-advised activity. Trashing your boss whilst he or she is within earshot is a serious CLM. (Also known as

CLB: Career Limiting Behavior.)

Adminisphere: the rarefied organizational layers beginning just above the rank and file. Decisions that fall from the adminisphere are often profoundly inappropriate or irrelevant to the problems they were designed to solve.

Flight risk: used to describe employees who are suspected of planning to leave the company or department soon.

404: someone who's clueless. From the World Wide Web error message "404: Not Found", meaning that the requested document could not be located. "Don't bother asking him…he's 404, man."

Ohnosecond: that minuscule fraction of time in which you realize that you've just made a *BIG* mistake.

Percussive maintenance: the fine art of whacking the crap out of an electronic device to get it to work again.

Prairie dogging: when someone yells or drops something loudly in a "cube farm" (an office full of cubicles) and everyone's heads pop up over the walls to see what's going on.

Assmosis: the process by which some people seem to absorb success and advancement by kissing up to the boss.

There are two ladies at work, sitting in a small office. A courier comes in and gives the one of the ladies flowers, sent by her husband. "That's nice" remarks the other lady. "No it isn't. This means I've got to stay awake and keep my legs up all night." She replied. "Why don't use just use a vase?"

HOLY OFFICE-In the beginning, there was the plan.

And then came the assumptions, and the assumptions were without form,

And the plan was without substance.

They giveth to the valley of the lepers. (err. workers).

And darkness was upon the face of the workers.

And they spoke amongst themselves and said, "It's a crock of shit, and it stinks." And the workers went unto their Supervisors and said, "It is a pail of dung, and we can't live with the stench."

And the Supervisors went unto their Managers and said, "It is a container of strong excrement, and none may abide by it."

And the Managers went unto their Directors and said, "It is a vessel of fertilizer, and none may abide it's strength."

And the Directors spoke among themselves, and said to one another, "It contains that which aids plant growth, and it is very strong."

And the Directors went to the Vice Presidents and said unto them, "It promotes growth, and it is very powerful."

And the Vice Presidents went to the President and said unto him, "This new plan

will actively promote growth and vigor of the
company with very powerful effects."
And the President looked upon the plan, and
said that it was good. And the plan became
policy.

How to take a day-long shit at work.
Memorize these definitions and pooping at
work will become a pure pleasure.
ESCAPEE Definition: A fart that slips out
while taking a leak at the urinal or forcing
poop in a stall. This is usually accompanied
by a sudden wave of panic/embarrassment.
This is similar to the hot flash you receive
when passing an unseen police car and
speeding. If you release an escapee, do not
acknowledge it. Pretend it did not happen. If
you are standing next to the farter at the
urinal, pretend that you did not hear it. No
one likes an escapee, it is uncomfortable for
all involved. Making a joke or laughing
makes both parties feel uneasy.
JAILBREAK (Used in conjunction with
escapee) Definition: When forcing poop,
several farts slip out at a machine gun's pace.
This is usually a side effect of diarrhea or a
hangover. If this should happen, do not panic.
Remain in the stall until everyone has left the

bathroom so to spare every one the awkwardness of what just occurred.

COURTESY FLUSH Definition: The act of flushing the toilet the instant the nose cone of the poop log hits the water and the poop is whisked away to an undisclosed location. This reduces the amount of air time the poop has to stink up the bathroom. This can help you avoid being caught doing the WALK OF SHAME.

WALK OF SHAME Definition: Walking from the stall, to the sink, to the door after you have just stunk-up the bathroom. This can be a very uncomfortable moment if someone walks in. As with all farts, it is best to pretend that the smell does not exist.

OUT OF THE CLOSET POOPER Definition: A colleague who poops at work and is damn proud of it. You will often see an Out of the Closet Pooper enter the bathroom with a newspaper or magazine under their arm. Always look around the office for the Out of the Closet pooper before entering the bathroom.

THE POOPING FRIENDS NETWORK (PFN) Definition: A group of coworkers who band together to ensure emergency pooping goes off with-out incident. This group can help you to monitor the whereabouts of OUT

OF THE CLOSET POOPERS and identify SAFE HAVENS.

SAFE HAVEN Definition: A seldom used bathroom somewhere in the building where you can least expect visitors. Try floors that are predominantly of the opposite sex. This will reduce the odds of a pooper of your sex entering the bathroom.

TURD BURGLAR Definition: A pooper who does not realize that you are in the stall and tries to force the door open. This is one of the most shocking and vulnerable moments that occur when taking a dump at work. If this occurs, remain in the stall until the TURD BURGLAR leaves. This way you will avoid all uncomfortable eye contact.

CAMO-COUGH Definition: A phony cough which alerts all new entrants into the bathroom that you are in a stall. This can be used to cover-up a WATERMELON or to alert potential TURD BURGLARS. Very effective when used in conjunction with an ASTAIRE. ASTAIRE Definition: A subtle toe-tap that is used to alert potential TURD BUR GLARS that you are occupying a stall. This will remove all doubt that the stall is occupied. If you hear an ASTAIRE, leave the bath-room immediately so the pooper can poop in peace.

WATERMELON Definition: A turd that creates a loud splash when hit-ting the toilet water. This is also an embarrassing incident. If you feel a WATERMELON coming on, create a diversion. See CAMO-COUGH.

HAVANA OMELET Definition: A load of diarrhea that creates a series of loud splashes in the toilet water. Often accompanied by an escapee. Try using a CAMO-COUGH with an ASTAIRE.

UNCLE TED Definition: A bathroom user who seems to linger around forever. Could spend extended lengths of time in front of the mirror or sit-ting on the pot. An UNCLE TED makes it difficult to relax while on the crapper, as you should always wait to drop your load when the bathroom is empty. This benefits you as well as the other bathroom attendees.

FLY BY Definition: The act of scouting out a bathroom before pooping. Walk in, check for other poopers. If there are others in the bathroom, leave and come back again. Be careful not to become a FRE-QUENT FLYER. People may become suspicious if they catch you constantly going into the bathroom.

CRACK WHORE Definition: A crapper that has seen more ass than a Greyhound Bus.

Tell-tale signs of CRACK WHORE include pubes, piss stains and shit streaks. Avoid CRACK WHORES at all cost. Try finding out when the janitor cleans each particular bathroom. Don't forget, a CRACK WHORE can become a SAFE HAVEN.

Forget the "I LOVE YOU" virus. There is a new virus going around called WORK. If you receive any sort of work, whether via e-mail, Internet, or simply handed to you by a colleague, do not open it. Those who have opened work have found that their social life is deleted and their brain ceases to function properly. If you do encounter work via e-mail or are faced with any work at all, then to purge the virus send an e-mail to your boss with the words 'This is too much for me. I'm going out for a while. This better not be here when I get back.' Your brain should automatically delete the work. If you receive work in paper document form, simply lift the document using your left hand and drag the work to your trash can, leave it there and it will be automatically removed at a later date. Send this message to all your friends in your address book. If you do not have any friends in your address book, then the WORK virus has already corrupted your life and you should seek help.

---

11 Reasons for going to work naked

11. No one ever steals your chair.
10. You now get two or more body areas to give you "bad hair day."
9. Diverts attention from the fact that you also came to work drunk.
8. People stop stealing your pens after they've seen where you keep them.
7. So that-with a little help from Muzak- you can add "Exotic Dancer" to your exaggerated resume.
6. You want to see if it's like the dream.
5. To stop those creepy guys in Marketing from looking down your blouse.
4. "I'd love to chip in, but I left my wallet in my pants."
3. Inventive way to finally meet that special person in Human Resources.
2. Can take advantage of computer monitor radiation to work on your tan. ..and (drum roll) the number one reason to Go To Work Naked:
1.Your boss is always yelling, "I wanna see your ass in here by 8:00!"

Signs Your Co-Worker is a Hacker:

-Everyone who ticks him or her off gets a $26,000 phone bill. -Has won the Publisher's Clearing House Sweepstakes three years running. -When asked for their phone number, they give it in hex.
-Seems strangely calm whenever the office LAN goes down. -Somehow gets HBO on their PC at work. -Mumbled, "Oh, puh-leeeez!" 295 times during the movie "The Net." -Massive 401k contribution made in half-cent increments. -Their video dating profile lists "public-key encryption" among turn ons. -Instead of the "Welcome" voice on AOL, you overhear, "Good Morning, Mr. 'n Mrs. President."
-You hear them murmur, "Let's see you use that VISA card now, Professor "I-Don't-Give-A's-In-Computer-Science!" -He gets confidential memos from NATO, The Pentagon, and Microsoft.

Your definitely a consultant if...

1. The first thing you do in the morning, before lunch, after lunch, before dinner, after dinner and before bed is check your voice mail.
2. You have more than one e-mail address.
3. You have 3 or more voicemails: Home, Office, and Client.
4. You sleep well on planes.
5. Your boss visiting you from out of town means a free meal.
6. You have ever expensed baseball tickets as team building.
7. You have ever creatively expensed gambling debts.
8. You have expensed cab rides to places you have never been.
9. You know the Avis car rental agent by first name.
10. You habitually check your e-mail every 5 minutes.
11. You can hold an entire conversation in acronyms and completely understand it.
12. You have ever had a meeting over a speaker phone.
13. You look forward to those little mints the maids leave you

14. Your idea of relaxing is only an 8 hour day.

15. Two Words: Alternative Travel

16. You can identify where other consultants are from by their laptop bags.

17. You only put on a suit in the office, not at the client's.

18. A home cooked meal means McDonalds down the street from your apartment.

19. You can identify at least 10 different types of airplanes by sight.

20. If you look for opportunities to expense things just to build frequent flyer miles.

21. If "Utilization" means anything to you.

22. You put a palm pilot on your Christmas list

23. If you have more phone numbers than fingers (i.e., home, home VM office, office direct, office VM, office fax, pager, cell phone, client, client VM, client fax, etc.)

24. A relaxing evening at home consists of catching up on administrative stuff

25. The words "Non-compliant" get a chuckle out of you.

26. You think of training as a place to pick up women

27. You have read all the Dilbert books.

28. You know the flight schedules of most major airlines

29. In one call you have asked your travel agent to quote you the most expensive price for one flight and then the cheapest price for another

30. You're still waiting for that great laptop they promised you when you signed.

31. You have friends who graduated with you and are still looking for jobs, while you constantly ignore calls from headhunters offering you a 20% raise.

32. You have never spent a full day in your 'home' office.

33. You've bribed your staffing coordinator to get the engagement you wanted.

34. You move your belongings into storage and get rid of your apartment so you have no expenses.

35. Mentoring means free lunches.

36. Counseling means free lunches.

37. Meetings mean more free lunches with the added bonus of happy hours.

38. Technical Support knows you by first name.

39. You pick a project based on whether or not it is business casual.

40. Team building is how last night's bar tab gets expensed.

41. You think of the quarterly meeting as a place to pick up women

42. You wake up in a motel and honestly don't know what city you're in.
43. You have a TracBall induced thumb callous.

One day an expert in time management was speaking to a group of business students and, to drive home a point, used an illustration the students will never forget. As this man stood in front of the group of high-powered overachievers, he said, "Okay, time for a quiz." Then he pulled out a one-gallon, wide-mouthed mason jar and set it on a table in front of him. Then he produced about a dozen fist-sized rocks and carefully placed them, one at a time, into the jar. When the jar was filled to the top and no more rocks would fit inside, he asked, "Is this jar full?" Everyone in the class said, "Yes." Then he said, "Really?" He reached under the table and pulled out a bucket of gravel. Then he dumped some gravel in and shook the jar causing pieces of gravel to work themselves down into the spaces between the big rocks. Then he asked the group once more, "Is the jar full?" By this time the class was on to him. "Probably not," one of them answered. "Good!" he replied. He reached under the table and brought out a bucket of sand. He started dumping the sand in, and it went into all the spaces left between the rocks and the gravel. Once more he asked the question, "Is this jar full?" "No!" the class shouted. Once again he said, "Good!" Then he grabbed a pitcher of water and began to pour it in until the jar was filled to the brim. Then he looked up at the class and asked, "What is the point of this illustration?" One eager beaver raised his hand and said, "The point is, no matter how full your schedule is, if you try really hard, you can always fit some more things into it!" "No," the speaker replied, "that's not the point. The truth this illustration teaches us is: If you don't put the big rocks in first, you'll never get them in at all." What are the "'big rocks'" in your life? Time with your loved ones? Your faith? Your dreams? A worthy cause? Remember to put these BIG ROCKS in first or you'll never get them in at all. So, tonight or in the morning when you are reflecting on this short story, ask yourself this question: What are the "big rocks'" in my life? Then, put those in your jar first.

KPMG Canada to Merge With the Vatican
VATICAN CITY —- In a surprise
announcement, Spencer Lanthier, chairman
of KPMG in Canada, announced that KPMG
Canada will be leaving KPMG International
and merging with the Vatican which is a
division of the Holy Roman Catholic Church.
The new firm will be called KPM-Jesus LLP.
"We feel that this is an exciting move for the
partnership." said Lanthier. "The Vatican's
huge client base combined with the
infallibility of their CEO is just what the
doctor ordered." Both organizations said they
expect few client conflicts, minimal
operational overlap and a smooth transition
to a merged firm. Lanthier said it hasn't been
determined how much administrative
restructuring or torturing of heretics is
needed. In a public statement, His Holiness
Pope John Paul II said that his main concern
was that KPMG employees might have a
hard time getting used to the Catholic
Church's dress code. KPMG Vice-Chairman,
Hugh Bessel, assured his Holiness that
KPMG Canada is an organization that "easily
accepts change", adding , "You know at first,
I thought this funny hat might be a problem,
but the chicks really dig it!" KPMG Canada's
Vice-Chairman, David Knight, currently

under threat of excommunication, referred to the proposed merger as the demonic spawn of an unholy union. Under the new merger plan, Lanthier will become "The Most Holy and Venerable Cardinal Lanthier of the Kingsway". Mr. Bessel will become Archbishop—Mergers and Inquisitions. Pete Masso, former CFO of KPMG will now be Cardinal of Finance and Collections.

Work Credo
Never give me work in the morning. Always wait until 4:00 and then bring it to me. The challenge of a deadline is so very refreshing If it's really a rush job, run in and interrupt me every 10 minutes to inquire how it's going. That helps. Or even better, hover behind me, advising me at every keystroke. Always leave without telling anyone where you're going. It gives me a chance to be creative when someone asks where you are. If my arms are full of papers, boxes, books, or supplies, don't open the door for me. I need to learn how to function as a paraplegic and opening doors with no arms is good training. If you give me more than one job to do, don't tell me which is the priority. I am psychic. Do your best to keep me late. I adore this office and really have nowhere to

go or anything to do. I have no life beyond work. If a job I do pleases you, keep it a secret. If that gets out, it could mean a pro motion. If you don't like my work, tell everyone. I like my name to be popular in conversations. I was born to be whipped. If you have special instructions for a job, don't write them down. In fact, save them until the job is almost done. No use confusing me with useful information. Never introduce me to the people you're with. I have no right to know anything. In the corporate food chain, I am plankton. When you refer to them later, my shrewd deductions will identify them. Be nice to me only when the job I'm doing for you could really change your life and send you straight to manager's hell. Tell me all your little problems. No one else has any and it's nice to know someone is less fortunate. I especially like the story about having to pay so much taxes on the bonus check you received for being such a good manager. Wait until my yearly review and THEN tell me what my goals SHOULD have been. Give me a mediocre performance rating with a cost of living increase. I'm not here for the money anyway.

Chapter 9. - LAWYERS

A local United Way office realized that the organization had never received a donation from the town's most successful lawyer. The person in charge of contributions called him to persuade him to contribute.

"Our research shows that out of a yearly income of at least $500,000, you give not a penny to charity. Wouldn't you like to give back to the community in some way?"

The lawyer mulled this over for a moment and replied, "First, did your research also show that my mother is dying after a long terminal illness, and has doctor bills and medical bills that are several times her annual income?"

Embarrassed, the United Way rep mumbled, "Um ... no."

The lawyer interrupts, "or that my brother, a disabled veteran, is blind and confined to a wheelchair?"

The stricken United Way rep began to stammer out an apology, but was interrupted again.

"or that my sister's husband died in a traffic accident," the lawyer's voice rising in indignation, "leaving her penniless with three children?!"

The humiliated United Way rep, completely beaten, said simply, "I had no idea..."
On a roll, the lawyer cut him off once again, "So if I don't give any money to them, why should I give any to you?"

GRANDMA IN COURT

Lawyers should never ask a Southern grandma a question if they aren't prepared for the answer.

In a trial, a Southern small-town prosecuting attorney called his first
witness, a grandmotherly, elderly woman to the stand.

He approached her and asked, "Mrs. Jones, do you know me?"

She responded, "Why, yes, I do know you , Mr. Williams.

I've known you since you were a young boy, and frankly, you've been a big disappointment to me.

You lie, you cheat on your wife, and you manipulate people and talk about them behind their backs.

You think you're a big shot when you haven't the brains to realize you never will amount to anything more than a two-bit paper pusher. Yes, I know you."

The lawyer was stunned! Not knowing what else to do, he pointed across the room and asked,
"Mrs. Jones, do you know the defense attorney?"
She again replied, "Why, yes, I do. I've known Mr. Bradley since he was a youngster, too.
He's lazy, bigoted, and he has a drinking problem.
He can't build a normal relationship with anyone and his law practice is one of the worst in the entire state.
Not to mention he cheated on his wife with three different women. One of them was your wife.
Yes, I know him." The defense attorney almost died. The judge asked both counselors to approach the bench and, in a very quiet voice, said, "If either of you fucking idiots asks her if she knows me, I'll send you to the electric chair "

The Gate is Broken. St. Peter was checking the gate between Heaven and Hell and found one of the hinges was broken. He walked over to the pit and yelled down at the devil. The devil swaggers up says, "What do you want?" "The hinge is broken and it's your turn to fix it." The devil says, "Ah, I am a bit busy and don't have anyone to spare for the job right now." Peter gets a bit miffed at this and says, "Look, we have an agreement, and it's your turn to fix the gate." The devil responded, "Ah…Sorry Pete, it's our peak season and there just isn't anyone around for this just now." St. Peter turned red and exclaimed, "Ok, if that's the way you want it, we'll sue." A big grin broke out on the devil's face. "Oh yeah…sure you are…and just where are you going to find a lawyer up there?"

A guy walks into a post office one day to see a middle-aged, balding man standing at the counter methodically placing "Love" stamps on bright pink envelopes with hearts all over them. The balding man then takes out a per fume bottle and starts spraying them all. His curiosity getting the better of him, he goes up to the balding man and asks him what he is doing. The man says, "I'm sending out 1,000 Valentine cards signed, 'Guess who?'" "But why?" asks the man. "I need the business I'm a divorce lawyer."

A lawyer defending a man accused of burglary tried this creative defense: "My client merely inserted his arm into the window and removed a few trifling articles. His arm is not himself, and I fail to see how you can punish the whole individual for an offense committed by his limb." "Well put," the judge replied. "Using your logic, I sentence the defendant's arm to one year's imprisonment. He can accompany it or not, as he chooses." The defendant smiled. With his lawyer's assistance he detached his artificial limb, laid it on the bench, and walked out.

A lawyer got married to a woman who had previously been married 13 times. On their wedding night, they settled into the bridal suite at their hotel and the bride said to her new groom, "Please, promise to be gentle. I am still a virgin." This puzzled the groom since, after 12 marriages, he thought that at least one of her husbands would have been able to per form. He asked his new bride to explain the phenomenon. She responded: My first husband was a Sales Representative who spent the entire marriage telling me, in grandiose terms, how great it was going to be. My second husband was from Software

Services; he was never quite sure how it was supposed to function, but he promised he would send me the documentation. My third husband was from Field Services and repeatedly said that everything was diagnostically OK, but couldn't get the system up. My fourth husband was from Educational Services, and you know the old saying—'Those who CAN, DO; those who can't, teach."

My fifth husband was from the Telemarketing Department. He knew he had the order, but he wasn't quite sure when he was going to be able to deliver. My sixth husband was an Engineer. He told me that he under stood the basic process but needed three years to research, implement, and design a new state-of-the-art method. My seventh husband was from Finance and administration. He knew how, but he just wasn't sure whether it was his job or not. My eighth husband was from Standards and Regulations, and he told me that they met the minimum standards but regulations weren't clear on how to do it. My ninth husband was a Marketing Manager. Even though he had the product he just wasn't sure how to position it. My tenth husband was a psychiatrist. All he ever wanted to do was talk about it. My eleventh husband was a gynecologist, and all he ever wanted to do was look at it. My twelfth husband was a stamp collector, and all he ever wanted to do was…Oh God I miss him! So now I've married you, and I'm really excited. Why is that," asked the lawyer. Well, it should be obvious! You're a lawyer! I just know I'm going to get screwed this time!"

A man calls his lawyer. The lawyer's admin asst. picks up the phone and explains that the lawyer is dead. The man hangs up. The next day, the man calls his lawyer again. Again the secretary explains that the lawyer is dead. The man hangs up. The following day, the man calls his lawyer yet again. This time the secretary gets angry and says, "Look, I've told you twice already. Your lawyer is dead. Why do you keep calling?" "I just like to hear it," responded the caller.

A secretary, a paralegal and a partner in a downtown law firm (which shall remain nameless) are walking threw a park on their way to lunch when they find an antique oil lamp. They rub it and a Genie comes out in a puff of smoke. The Genie says, "I usually only grant three wishes, so I'll give each of you just one." "Me first! Me first!", says the secretary. "I want to be in the Bahamas, driving a speedboat, without a care in the world." Poof! She's gone. In astonishment, "Me next! Me next!", says the paralegal, "I want to be in Hawaii, relaxing on the beach with my personal masseuse, an endless cup of pina coladas and the love of my life." Poof! He's gone. "You're next," the Genie says to the partner. The partner says, "I want those two back in the office after lunch."

Billable Hours
A lawyer dies in a car accident on his 40th birthday and finds himself greeted at the Pearly Gates by a brass band. Saint Peter runs over, shakes his hand and says "Congratulations!!!"

"Congratulations for what?" asks the lawyer.

"Congratulations for what?!?!?" says Saint Peter. "We're celebrating the fact that you lived to be 176 years old."

"But that's not true," says the lawyer. "I only lived to be forty."

"That's impossible," says Saint Peter. "We've added up your time sheets."

— — — — — — — — — —

Chapter 10. - Q & A

Question: What is it when a man talks dirty to a woman? Answer: Sexual harassment.
Question: What is it when a woman talks dirty to a man? Answer: $3.99 a minute.
Question: What do you call a Florida gynecologist? Answer: A spreader of old wives' tails...
Question: Why do women prefer old gynecologists? Answer: They have shaky hands!
Question: What do a Divorce in Alabama, a Tornado in Kansas, and a Hurricane in Florida have in common? Answer: Somebody's fixin' to lose them a trailer house.
Question. What's the fastest way to a man's heart? Answer. Through his chest with a sharp knife.
Question: Why are men and parking spaces alike? Answer: Because all the good ones are gone and the only ones left are disabled.
Question: Why are men like public toilets? Answer: They're always vacant, engaged or full of shit.
Question: What have men and floor tiles got in common? Answer: If you lay them

properly the first time, you can walk all over them for life.

Question: What are two reasons why men don't mind their own business? Answer: 1. No mind. 2. No business.

Question: Did you hear about the banker who's a great lover? Answer: He knows first-hand the penalty for early withdrawal.

Question: Why are men like laxatives? Answer: They irritate the shit out of you.

Question: Why do men name their penises? Answer: Because they want to be on a first-name basis with the person who makes all their decisions.

Question: Why is it so hard for women to find men that are sensitive, caring, and good-looking? Answer: Because those men already have boyfriends.

Question: What's the difference between a porcupine and a BMW? Answer: Porcupines have pricks on the outside.

Question: What is a man's view of safe sex? Answer: A padded headboard.

Question: How do men sort their laundry? Answer: "Filthy" and "Filthy but Wearable".

Question: Why were men given larger brains than dogs? Answer: So they wouldn't hump women's legs at cocktail parties.

Question: How do you save a man from drowning? Answer: Take your foot off his head.

Question: What do men and beer bottles have in common? Answer: They're both empty from the neck up.

Question: Why did God create men? Answer: Vibrators can't mow the lawn.

Question: Why do female black widow spiders kill the males after mating? Answer: To stop the snoring before it starts.

Question: Why do bachelors like smart women? Answer: Opposites attract.

Question: What's the difference between a new husband and a new dog? Answer: After a year the dog is still excited to see you.

Question: What's a man's idea of foreplay? Answer: Half an hour of begging.

Question: What did the lesbian frog say to the other lesbian frog? Answer: They're right! We do taste like chicken!

Question: What do a Christmas tree and priests have in common? Answer: Their balls are just for decoration.

Question: How do you find a Blind Man in a nudist colony? Answer: It's not hard.

Question: What's the difference between a girlfriend and a wife? Answer: 45 lbs.

Question: What's the difference between a boyfriend and a husband? Answer: 45 minutes

Question: What's the difference between a 90's woman and a computer?
Answer: A 90's woman won't accept a three and a half inch floppy.

Question: Why do men find it difficult to make eye contact? Answer: Breasts don't have eyes.

Question: What's the difference between erotic and kinky? Answer: Erotic is when you use a feather. Kinky is when you use the whole chicken.

Question: What is the difference between medium and rare? Answer: Six inches is medium, eight inches is rare.

Question: What do you call a dog with no legs? Answer: It doesn't matter. He won't come anyway.

Question: What is a zebra? Answer: 26 sizes larger than an "A" bra.

Question: What's the difference between an oral thermometer and a rectal thermometer? Answer: The taste.

Question: Why do bagpipers walk when they play? Answer: They're trying to get away from the noise.

Question: Why do gorillas have big nostrils?
Answer: Because they have big fingers.

Question: Which sexual position produces the ugliest children? Answer: Ask your mom.

Question: What is the quickest way to clear out a men's restroom? Answer: Say, "Nice dick."

Question: How do you know you're leading a sad life? Answer: When a nymphomaniac tells you, "Let's just be friends."

Question: Are birth control pills deductible? Answer: Only if they don't work.

Question: What did one saggy boob say to the other saggy boob? Answer: If we don't get some support soon, people are going to think we're nuts.

Question: Why don't bunnies make noise when they make love? Answer: Because they have cotton balls.

Question: What do you get when you cross an Owl and a Rooster? Answer: A cock that stays up all night.

Question: Moms have Mother's Day, Fathers have Father's Day. What do single guys have? Answer: Palm Sunday

Question: What do you call a ninety year old man who can still masturbate? Answer: Miracle Whip.

Question: What has a whole bunch of little balls and screws old ladies? Answer: A bingo machine.

Question: How do you get a University graduate with an MBA to get off your porch? Answer : You pay for the pizza!!

Question. Where do you get virgin wool from? Answer. Ugly sheep.

Question. How do you make a dog drink? Answer. Put it in a blender.

Question. How do you change a woman's mind? Answer. Buy her another beer.

Question: How do crazy people go through the forest? Answer: They take the psycho path.

Question: How do you get holy water? Answer: Boil the hell out of it.

Question: What did the fish say when he hit a concrete wall? Answer: "Dam."

Question: What do Eskimos get from sitting on the ice too long? Answer: Polaroids.

Question: What do prisoners use to call each other? Answer: Cell phones.

Question: What do you call a boomerang that doesn't work? Answer: A stick.

Question: What do you call cheese that isn't yours? Answer: Nacho Cheese.

Question: What do you call Santa's helpers? Answer: Subordinate Clauses.

Question: What do you get from a pampered cow? Answer: Spoiled milk.

Question: What do you get when you cross a snowman with a vampire? Answer: Frostbite.

Question: What has four legs, is big, green, fuzzy, and if it fell out of tree would kill you? Answer: A pool table.

Question: What lies at the bottom of the ocean and twitches? Answer: A nervous wreck.

Question: What's the difference between roast beef and pea soup? Answer: Anyone can roast beef.

Question: Where do you find a dog with no legs? Answer: Right where you left him.

Question: Why are there so many Smiths in the phone book? Answer: They all have phones.

Question: What is long and hard to a blondish (check the roots)? Answer: Grade 4

Question: Why did God create alcohol? Answer: So ugly people have a chance to have sex.

Question: What did the blondish say when she found out she was pregnant? Answer: "Are you sure it's mine?"

Question: What's the difference between beer nuts and deer nuts? Answer: Beer nuts are a $1.25 but deer nuts are always under a buck.

Question: What three two-letter words denote "small"? Answer: "Is it in?"

Question: What is the difference between a tick and a lawyer? Answer: A tick falls off you when you die.

Question: What's the definition of mixed emotions? Answer: When you see your mother-in-law backing off a cliff in your new car.

Question: What do call a lawyer with an IQ of 50? Answer: Your Honor

Question: Why does Mike Tyson cry during sex? Answer: Mace will do that to you

Chapter 11. - REDNECK EMAILS

In the backwoods of the Blue Ridge Mountains, the redneck's wife went into labor in the middle of the night, and the doctor was called in to assist in the delivery. Since there was no electricity, the doctor handed the father-to-be a lantern and said, "Here, you hold this high so I can see what I'm doing." Soon, a baby boy was brought into the world. "Whoa there, " said the doctor. "Don't be in a rush to put the lantern down...I think there's yet another one to come." Sure enough, within minutes he had delivered a baby girl. "No, no, don't be in a great hurry to be putting down that lantern...It seems there's yet another one in there!" cried the doctor. The Redneck scratched his head in bewilderment, and asked the doctor, "Do you think it's the light that's attraction' 'em?"

Dear Redneck Son #3 and a half;
I'm writing this letter real slow 'cuse I know you can't read fast even with your good eye. We don't live where we did when you left home. Your dad read in the newspaper that most accidents happen within 20 miles from your home, so we moved. I won't be able to send you the address because the last Arkansas family that lived here took the house numbers when they moved so that they wouldn't have to change their address. This place is really nice. It even has a washing machine. I'm not sure it works so well though: last week I put a load in and pulled the chain and haven't seen them since. The weather isn't bad here. It only rained twice last week; the first time for three days and the second time for four days. Your newphew/uncle Bubba only got struck three times by lighten too. Your Aunt/sister Thelma lost the bet on that one! About that coat you wanted me to send you, your Uncle Stanley said it would be too heavy to send in the mail with the buttons on, so we cut them off and put them in the pockets. John locked his keys in the car yester day. We were really worried because it took him two hours to get me and your father out. Your sister had a baby this morning; but I haven't found out

what it is yet so I don't know if you're an aunt or an uncle. The baby looks just like your brother. Three of your friends went off a bridge in a pick-up truck. Ralph was driving. He rolled down the window and swam to safety. Your other two friends were in back. They drowned because they couldn't get the tail-gate down. There isn't much more news at this time. Nothing much has happened.
Love, Mom
P.S. I was going to send you some money but the envelope was already sealed.

Technology for Country Folk...
1. LOG ON: Makin a wood stove hotter.
2. LOG OFF: Don't add no more wood.
3. MONITOR: Keepin an eye on the wood stove.
4. DOWNLOAD: Gettin the firewood off the truck.
5. MEGA HERTZ: When yer not kerful gettin the farwood.
6. FLOPPY DISC: Whatcha git from tryin to carry too much farwood.
7. RAM: That thar thing whut splits the farwood.
8. HARD DRIVE: Gettin home in the winter time.

9. PROMPT: Whut the mail ain't in the winter time.

10. WINDOWS: Whut to shut wen it's cold outside.

11. SCREEN: Whut to shut wen it's black fly season.

12. BYTE: Whut them dang flys do.

13. CHIP: Munchies fer the TV.

14. MICRO CHIP: Whut's in the bottom of the munchie bag.

15. MODEM: Whut cha did to the hay fields.

16. DOT MATRIX: Old Dan Matrix's wife.

17. LAP TOP: Whar the kitty sleeps.

18. KEYBOARD: Whar ya hang the dang keys.

19. SOFTWARE: Them dang plastic forks and knifs.

20. MOUSE: Whut eats the grain in the barn.

21. MAINFRAME: Holds up the barn roof.

22. PORT: Fancy Flatlander wine.

23. ENTER: Northerner talk fer "C'mon in y'all."

24. RANDOM ACCESS MEMORY: Wen ya cain't 'member whut ya paid fer the rifle when yore wife asks.

25. MOUSE PAD: That hippie talk fer the rat hole.

REDNECK COUNTY DRIVER'S LICENSE APPLICATION

Last name: _____

(if uncertain put down the name used on TV show COPS)

First name: (Check appropriate box) [_]
Billy-Bob [_] Bobby-Sue [_] Billy-Joe [_]
Bobby-Jo [_] Billy-Ray [_] Bobby-Ann [_]
Billy-Sue [_] Bobby-Lee [_] Billy-Mae [_]
Bobby-Ellen [_] Billy-Jack [_] Bobby-Beth

Age: _____ (if unsure, guess)

Sex: _____ M _____ F _____ Both _____ Not sure

Shoe Size: _____ Left _____ Right

Occupation: (Check appropriate box)
[_] Sr. Junk Yard Consultant [_] Moonshine Maker [_] Farmer [_] Mechanic [_] Hair Dresser [_] Waitress [_] Unemployed [_] Dirty Politician

Spouse's Name:

_____

2nd Spouse's Name:

_____

3rd Spouse's Name:

_____

Lover's Name:

_____

2nd Lover's Name:

_____

Relationship to spouse: (Check appropriate box)
[_] Sister [_] Aunt [_] Brother [_] Uncle [_]
Mother [_] Son [_] Father [_] Daughter [_]
Cousin [_] Pet

Number of children living in household: ____
Number of children living in shed: ____

Number that are yours: ____
(don't forget to count the ones under the porch)

Mother's Name: _____

Father's Name: _____
(If not sure, leave blank)

Education: 1 2 3 4 (Circle highest grade completed)

Do you [_] own or [_] rent your mobile home? (Check appropriate box)

Total number of vehicles you own ___
Number of vehicles that still crank ___
Number of vehicles in front yard ___
Number of vehicles in back yard ___
Number of vehicles on cement blocks

Where you keep them firearms:
__ truck ___ kitchen ___ bedroom ___
bathroom ____ shed

Model and year of your pickup:
_____ 194_

Do you have a gun rack? [_] Yes [_] No;
 If no, please explain:_____

Newspapers/magazines you subscribe to:
[_] The National Enquirer [_] The Globe [_]
TV Guide [_] Soap Opera Digest [_] Rifle
and Shotgun

Number of times you've seen a UFO ___
Number of times you've seen Elvis ___
Number of times you've seen Elvis in a UFO

How often do you bathe:
[_] Weekly [_] Monthly [_] Not Applicable

Color of teeth: [_] Yellow [_] Brownish-
Yellow [_] Brown [_] Black [_] N/A [_]
Teeth?

Brand of chewing tobacco you prefer:
[_] Red-Man

How far is your home from a paved road?
[_] 1 mile [_] 2 miles [_] don't know

Getting ahead
Two rednecks decided that they weren't
going anywhere in life and thought they
should go to college to get ahead. The first
goes in to see the counselor, who tells him to
take Math, History, and Logic. "What's
Logic?" the first redneck asks. The professor
answers by saying, "Let me give you an
example. Do you own a weedeater?"
"I sure do." "Then I can assume, using logic,
that you have a yard," replied the professor.
"That's real good!" says the redneck. The

professor continues, "Logic will also tell me that since you have a yard, you also own a house." Impressed, the redneck says, "Amazin!" "And since you own a house, logic dictates that you have a wife." "That's Betty Mae! This is incredible!" The redneck is obviously catching on. "Finally, since you have a wife, logically I can assume that you are heterosexual," said the professor. "You're absolutely right! Why that's the most fascinatin' thing I ever heard! I can't wait to take that logic class!!" The redneck, proud of the new world opening up to him, walks back into the hallway, where his friend is still waiting. "So what classes are ya takin'?" asks the friend. "Math, History, and Logic!" replies the first redneck. "What in tarnation is logic???" asked his friend. "Let me give you an example. Do ya own a weedeater?" asked the first redneck. "No," his friend replied. "Fag."

A young ventriloquist is touring the clubs and stops to entertain at a bar in a small town. He's going through his usual stupid Redneck jokes, when a big burly guy in the audience stands up and says "I've heard just about enough of your smart ass hillbilly jokes; we ain't all stupid around here."

Flustered, the ventriloquist begins to apologize, when the big guy pipes up, "You stay out of this mister, I'm talking to the little fella on your knee!" Did you hear about the South Carolina redneck who passed away and left his entire estate in trust for his beloved widow? She can't touch it till she's fourteen. What's the most popular pick-up line in Alabama? Nice tooth wanna see mine?

Emily Sue passed away and Bubba called 911. The 911 operator told Bubba that she would send someone out right away. "Where do you live?" asked the operator. Bubba replied, "At the end of Euphoria Drive." The operator asked, "Can you spell that for me?" There was a long pause and finally Bubba said, "How 'bout if I drag her over to Oak Street and you pick her up there?"

How do you know when you're staying in a Kentucky hotel? When you call the front desk and say "I've gotta leak in my sink" and the person at the front desk says "go ahead."

How can you tell if a Texas redneck is married? There is dried chewing tobacco on both sides of his pickup truck.

Did you hear that they have raised the minimum drinking age in Tennessee to 32? It seems they want to keep alcohol out of the high schools!

What do they call reruns of "Hee Haw" in Mississippi? A documentary.

How many rednecks does it take eat a 'possum? Two. One to eat, and one to watch out for traffic.

Why did God invent armadillos? So that Texas rednecks can have 'pos sum on the halfshell.

Where was the toothbrush invented? Oklahoma. If it was invented any where else it would have been called teethbrush.

Arkansas State trooper pulls over a pickup truck on I-40. He says to the driver, "Got any ID?" The driver says, "Bout what?"

Did you hear about the $3,000,000 Tennessee State Lottery? The winner gets $3 a year for a million years.

Why did O. J. Simpson want to move to West Virginia? Everyone has the same DNA.

Did you hear that the governor's mansion in Little Rock, Arkansas burned down? Yep. Pert' near took out the whole trailer park.

A new law recently passed in North Carolina: When a couple gets divorced, they're still brother and sister.

What's the best thing to ever come out of Arkansas? I-40.

Two Mississippians are walking down different ends of a street toward each other, and one is carrying a sack. When they meet, one says, "Hey Tommy Ray, what'cha got in th' bag?" "Jus' some chickens." "If I guesses how many they are, can I have one?" "Shoot, ya guesses right and I'll give you both of them." "OK. Ummmmm…five?"

A Mississippian came home and found his house on fire. He rushed next door, telephoned the fire department and shouted, "Hurry over here.
My house is on fire!" "OK," replied the fireman, "how do we get there?" "Shucks,

don't you still have those big red trucks?"

Why do folks in Kentucky go to the movie theater in groups of 18 or more? 'Cuz 17 and under not admitted

CHAPTER 12. – MISCELLANEOUS

Dear Little Boy:

I have been watching you very closely to see if you have been good this year, and since you have, I will be telling my elves to make some goodies for me to leave under your tree at Christmas. I was going to bring you all the gifts from the "Twelve Days of Christmas", but we have had a little problem up here. The eleventh of the twelve fiddlers fiddling have all come down with VD from fiddling with the ten ladies dancing (one of the fiddlers fiddling didn't get VD cause he is gay). The eleven lords a leaping have knocked up the eight maids of milking, and the nine pipers playing have been arrested for doing weird things. Four calling birds, three French hens, two turtle doves, and the partridge in a pear tree have me up to my ass in bird shit. On top of all this, Mrs. Claus is going through her 80th season of menopause, eight of my reindeer are in heat, the elves have joined the Gay Liberation and those dumb-ass Poles have scheduled Christmas in Poland for the 5th of February. Sincerely, Santa Claus

It was a hot day in Minnesota. Heidi hung the wash out to dry, put a roast in the oven, then went downtown to pick up some dry cleaning. "Gootness, it's hot," she mused to herself as she walked down Main street. She passed by a tavern and thought, "Vy nodt?" so she walked in and took a seat at the bar. The bartender came up and asked her what she would like to drink. "Ya know," Heidi said, "it is so hot I tink I'll have myself zee cold beer." The bartender asked, "Anheuser Busch?" Helga blushed and replied "Vell bit dry butt fine, tanks, und how's yer pecker?"

LITTLE SILLY WILLY ON SEX
Little silly Willy walked into his dad's bedroom one day only catch him sit-ting on the side of his bed sliding on a condom. Johnny's father, in attempt to hide his full erection with a condom on it, bent over as if to look under the bed. Little silly Willy asked curiously "What ya doin dad?" His father quickly replied, "I thought I saw a rat go underneath the bed," to which Little silly Willy replied "What ya gonna do, fuck him?"
LIT TLE JOHNNY'S LITTLE LAMB The third grade teacher was teaching English and repeated for her class: "Mary had a little lamb, whose fleece was white as snow. And

everywhere that Mary went, the lamb was sure to go." She explained that this was an example of poetry, but could be changed to prose by changing the last line from "the lamb was sure to go"to the lamb went with her." A few days later she asked for an example of poetry or prose. Johnny raised his hand and recited, "Mary had a little pig, an ornery little runt. He stuck his nose in Mary's clothes, and smelled her little—" he stopped and asked the teacher if she wanted poetry or prose. "Prose!" the teacher said weakly. So Johnny said, "Asshole."

Bud and Jay were playing golf; Jay asked Bud for a match. Bud reached into his golf bag and pulled out a 12-inch BIC lighter. Jay: "Wow! Where did you get that monster?" Bud: "I got it from my genie." Jay: "You have a genie?" Bud: "Yes, he's right here in my golf bag." Jay: "Could I see him?" Bud opened his golf bag and out popped the genie. Jay: "I'm a good friend of your master. Will you grant me one wish?"
Genie: "Yes I will." So Jay asked the genie for a million bucks. The genie hopped back into the golf bag and left him standing there waiting for his million bucks. Suddenly, the sky begins to darken and the sound of a mil-

lion ducks flying overhead was heard. Jay said to Bud, "I asked for a million bucks, not ducks!" "Well" said Bud, "Do you really think I asked him for a 12-inch BIC?"

A judge asked a defendant to please stand. "You are charged with murdering a school teacher with a chain saw." From out in the audience a man shouted, "Lying bastard!" "Silence in the court!", the judge shouted back to the man. He turned to the defendant and said, "You are also charged with killing a paperboy with a shovel." "Tightwad!" blurted the man again. "Quiet!" yelled the judge who continued, "You are also charged with killing a mailman with an electric drill." "Son of a…" the man started to shout when the judge thundered back, "If you don't tell me reason for your outbursts right now, I will hold you in contempt!" So the man answered, "I've lived next to that man for ten years now, but do you think he ever had a tool when I needed to borrow one!"

The teacher decided to give a pop quiz on this week's spelling words. She asked the students to spell the words and use them in a sentence. Three of the words were HOTEL,

STIGMA and HOMOSEXUAL. Little
Johnny's answers were:
1. h-o-t-e-l—The president asked Monica to
keep their affair a secret, but Linda Tripp
made the ho-tel.
2. s-t-i-g-m-a—The president said to Monica,
"I want you to stigma cigar in your you-
know-what."
3. h-o-m-o-s-e-x-u-a-l—The president asked
Monica not to wear panties because he
thought it made the ho mo sexual. Little
Johnny was suspended.

An old woman went to visit her daughter and
she found her naked, waiting for her
husband. The mother asks the daughter:
"What are you doing naked?" The daughter
responds: "This is the dress of love." When
the mother returns home, she strips naked
and waits for her husband. When her husband
arrives, he asks her: "What are you doing
naked, woman?" She responds: "This is the
dress of love." And he said to her: "Well, go
iron it first."

An old man was sitting on his front porch
watching the sun rise. He sees the neighbor's
kid in his scouts uniform walk by carrying
something big under his arm. He yells out

"Hey boy, whatcha got there?" Boy yells back "Roll of chicken wire." Old man says "What you gonna do with that?" Boy says "They're gonna teach us to catch some chickens." Old man yells "You damn fool, you can't catch chickens with chicken wire!" Boy just laughs and keeps walking. That evening at sunset the boy comes walking by in the scouts uniform And, to the old man's surprise, he is dragging behind him the chicken wire with about 30 chickens caught in it. Same time next morning the old man is out watching the sun rise and he sees the boy in his uniform walk by carrying something kind of round in his hand. Old man yells out "Hey boy, whatcha got there?" Boy yells back "Roll of duck tape." Old man says "What you gonna do with that?" Boy says back "Scout master is gonna to teach us how catch some ducks." Old man yells back, "You damn fool, you can't catch ducks with duck tape!" Boy just laughs and keeps walking. That night around sunset the boy walks by coming home and to the old man's amazement he is trailing behind him the unrolled roll of duck tape with about 35 ducks caught in it. Same time next morning the old man sees the boy walking by carrying what looks like a long reed with something fuzzy on the end. Old man says "Hey boy, whatcha got there?" Boy says "It's pussy willow." Old man says "Wait for me, ...I'll get my old uniform and my hat."

The local bar was so sure that its bartender was the strongest man around that they offered a standing $1000 bet. The bartender would squeeze a lemon until all the juice ran into a glass, and hand the lemon to a patron. Anyone who could squeeze one more drop of juice out would win the money. Many people had tried over time (weightlifters, long shore men, etc.) but nobody could do it. One day this scrawny little man came in, wearing thick glasses and a polyester suit, and said in a tiny, squeaky voice, " I'd like to try the bet." After the laughter had died down, the bartender said OK, grabbed a lemon, and squeezed away. Then he handed the wrinkled remains of the rind to the little man. But the crowd's laughter turned to total silence as the man clenched his fist around the lemon and six drops fell into the glass. As the crowd cheered, the bar tender paid the $1000, and asked the little man, "What do you do for a living? Are you a lumberjack, a weightlifter, or what?" The man replied, "I work for the

IRS. and for another $1000 ya' wanna see me get blood from a turnip?

All the organs of the body were having a meeting, trying to decide who was in charge. "I should be in charge," said the brain, "because I run all the body's systems, so without me nothing would happen." "I should be in charge," said the heart, "because I circulate oxygen all over, so without me you'd all waste away." "I should be in charge," said the stomach, "because I process food and give all of you energy." "I should be in charge," said the rectum, "because I'm responsible for waste removal." All the other body parts laughed at the rectum and insulted him, so in a huff, he shut down tight. Within a few days, the brain had a terrible headache, the stomach was bloated, and the heart was toxic. Eventually the other organs gave in. They all agreed that the rectum should be the boss. The moral of the story? You don't have to be smart or important to be in charge...you just have to be an asshole.

Dr. BEER Solves your problem
SYMPTOM: Feet cold and wet.
FAULT: Glass being held at incorrect angle.
REMEDY: Rotate glass so that open end points toward ceiling.

SYMPTOM: Feet warm and wet.
FAULT: Improper bladder control.
REMEDY: Stand next to nearest dog, complain about house training.

SYMPTOM: Beer unusually pale and tasteless.
FAULT: Glass empty.
REMEDY: Get someone to buy you another beer.

Dr. BEER Solves your problem
SYMPTOM: Opposite wall covered with fluorescent lights.
FAULT: You have fallen over backward.
REMEDY: Have yourself chained to bar.

SYMPTOM: Mouth contains cigarette butts.
FAULT: You have fallen forward.
REMEDY: See above.

SYMPTOM: Beer tasteless, front of your shirt is wet.

FAULT: Mouth not open, or glass applied to wrong part of face.
REMEDY: Retire to restroom, practice in mirror.

Dr. BEER Solves your problem
SYMPTOM: Floor blurred.
FAULT: You are looking through bottom of empty glass.
REMEDY: Get someone to buy you another beer.

SYMPTOM: Floor moving.
FAULT: You are being carried out.
REMEDY: Find out if you are being taken to another bar.

SYMPTOM: Room seems unusually dark.
FAULT: Bar has closed.
REMEDY: Confirm home address with bartender, take taxi home.

———————————

THE UNABRIDGED CAR ACRONYMS
GUIDE:
AUDI
Accelerates Under Demonic Influence
Always Unsafe Designs Implemented
All Uninformed Drivers Insulted
All Unnecessary Devices Installed

BMW
Big Money Works
Bought My Wife
Brutal Money Waster

BUICK
Big Ugly Indestructible Car Killer

CHEVROLET
Can Hear Every Valve Rap On Long
Extended Trips Cheap, Hardly Efficient,
Virtually Runs On Luck Every Time

DODGE
Damn Old Dirty Gas Eater
Drips Oil, Drops Grease Everywhere

FORD
Fix Or Repair Daily
Found On Road, Dead
Fast Only Rolling Downhill

THE UNABRIDGED CAR ACRONYMS
GUIDE:
FIAT
Fucked In Acceleration Time

GM
General Maintenance
GMC Garage Man's Companion
Get Maintenance Contract

HONDA
Had One Never Did Again
Happy Owners Never Drove Autobahn

HYUNDAI
Hope You Understand Nothing's Drive able
And Inexpensive

MAZDA
Most Always Zipping Dangerously Along

OLDSMOBILE
Old Ladies Driving Slowly Make Others
Behind Infuriatingly Late Everyday.
Overpriced, Leisurely Driven Sedan Made Of
Buick's Irregular Leftover Equipment

SAAB
Send Another Automobile Back

TOYOTA
Too Often Yankees Overprice This Auto

VOLVO
Very Odd Looking Vehicular Object

VW
Virtually Worthless

A man lay sprawled across three entire seats in the posh theater. When the usher came by and noticed this, he whispered to the man, "Sorry, sir, but you're only allowed one seat." The man groaned but didn't budge. The usher became impatient. "Sir, if you don't get up from there I'm going to have to call the manager." Again, the man just groaned, which infuriated the usher who turned and marched briskly back up the aisle in search of his manager. In a few moments, both the usher and the manager returned and stood over the man. Together the two of them tried repeatedly to move him, but with no success. Finally, they summoned the police. The cop surveyed the situation briefly then asked, "All right buddy, what's your name?" "Bill," the man moaned. What's your address? the cop asked "15 Elm Ave."

replied the man. "What's your occupation?"
With pain in his voice Sam replied "Ceiling
repair." Both the cop and the usher look up in
realization.

A MORNING POEM (for non-morning
people)
I woke early one morning,
The earth lay cool and still
When suddenly a Robin
Perched on my window sill,
He sang a song a lullaby
So carefree and so gay,
That slowly all my troubles Began to go
away.
He sang of far off places
Of laughter and of fun,
It seemed his very singing,
Brought up the morning sun.
I stirred beneath my covers
Crept slowly out of bed,
And gently lowered the window
And crushed him, so he's dead.

An older woman was cleaning her attic with her cat by her side for company. Amongst the boxes and old papers she found a little lamp. She picked it up and wiped it off with her apron, when "POOF" out popped Genie. "I will grant you three wishes" proclaimed the Genie. The woman thought for a moment and said "I wish I was the most beautiful 20 year old woman in the world, I wish I had more money than I knew what to do with, and I wish you would turn my cat into the most handsome prince around." The Genie nodded and after a huge cloud of dust cleared the Genie was gone and so was the lamp. The woman looked at herself and she was certainly beautiful. She was surrounded with scads of money in large bills. She flung an armful in the air and watched it flutter down around her. She giggled with delight at the mountains of cash. Then she turned to look where her adoring cat once stood. There in the feline's place stood a tall, dark, handsome man with chiseled features. a washboard stomach, broad shoulders and a soccer player's tush. She walked over to him, he put his arms around her, brushed his hand upon her cheek, looked deep into her eyes and whispered softly. Now, aren't you sorry you had me neutered?

I worked for a while at a department store, selling sporting goods. As an employee of this particular department store you are sometimes required to make storewide pages, e.g., "I have a customer in hardware who needs assistance at the paint counter." One night, an employee wasn't thinking when he said over the intercom: "I have a customer by the balls in toys who needs assistance."

Bathroom Graffiti
If you can piss this high, join the fire department.
Beauty is only a light switch away.
I've decided that to raise my grades I must lower my standards.
If life is a waste of time, and time is a waste of life, then let's all get wasted together and have the time of our lives.
Remember, it's not, "How high are you?" it's "Hi, how are you?"
God made pot. Man made beer. Who do you trust?
Fighting for peace is like screwing for virginity.
No matter how good she looks, some other guy is sick and tired of put ting up with her shit.

At the feast of ego, everyone leaves hungry.
It's hard to make a comeback when you
haven't been anywhere.
Make love, not war. Hell, do both, get
married!
God is dead. -Nietzsche
Nietzsche is dead. –God

If voting could really change things, it would
be illegal.
A Woman's Rule of Thumb: If it has tires or
testicles, you're going to have trouble with it.
JESUS SAVES! But wouldn't it be better if
he had invested?
If pro is opposite of con, then what is the
opposite of progress? Congress!
Express Lane: five beers or less.

Three girls are sitting around talking about
the night before. First girl says, "I was so
drunk last night. I went home and blew
buckets". The second girl responded with,
"that's nothing. I was so drunk, I took off my
clothes before I got in my house". The third
girl said, "I was so drunk driving home, ran
into a mailbox, hit a telephone pole and
crashed into a tree". The second shook her
head and agreed that the third girl was the
drunkest. The first girl explained her

situation with, "You don't understand. Buckets is my dog".

Remember the first time going down?…………….. I was scared at first. It was very wide, and very long, and it angled straight down. I decided I had to try it once. I slowly and carefully eased myself onto it. It felt weird at first. Then I got used to it. I went up and down, and up and down on it. I was really loving it. BUT……. Now I ride on the department store escalators all the time!! (*admit it, you thought this was a dirty joke….hehehehe*)

A very large old building was being torn down in Chicago to make room for a new skyscraper. Due to its proximity to other buildings it could not be imploded and had to be dismantled floor by floor. While working on the 49th floor, two construction workers found a skeleton in a small closet behind the elevator shaft. They decided that they should call the police. When the police arrived they directed them to the closet and showed them the skeleton fully clothed and standing upright. They said "this could be Jimmy Hoffa or somebody really important."

Two days went by and the construction workers couldn't stand it any more, they had to know who they had found. They called the police and said, "We are the two guys who found the skeleton in the closet and we want to know if it was Jimmy Hoffa or somebody important." The police said, "It's not Jimmy Hoffa, but it was somebody kind of important." "Well, who was it?" The 1948 International Blondish Hide-and-Seek Champion.

Yo' Mama's so fat.......

Yo' Mama's so fat.......When she dances she makes the band skip.

Yo' Mama's so fat.......She got flesh eating disease the Doctor gave her 13 years to live.

Yo' Mama's so fat.......She puts mayonnaise on her aspirin.

Yo' Mama's so fat.......Her ass has it's own congress man.

Yo' Mama's so fat.......Her cereal bowl came with a life guard.

Yo' Mama's so fat.......When she goes to the zoo the elephants throw her peanuts.

Yo' Mama's so fat.......Her high school graduation picture was an aerial photograph from the Hubbell Telescope.

Yo' Mama's so fat.......Her driver's license says "picture continued on other side".
Yo' Mama's so fat.......when she swims in the ocean it automatically becomes high tide.
Yo' Mama's so fat.......The back of her neck looks like a package of hot dogs.
Yo' Mama's so fat.......All the restaurants say "maximum of 240 patrons or Yo' Mama"
Yo' Mama's so fat.......When she ran away they had to use all sides of the milk carton.
Yo' Mama's so fat.......She was born with a silver shovel in her mouth.
Yo' Mama's so fat.......She's got smaller fat women orbiting her.
Yo' Mama's so fat.......I had to take a train and two buses to get on her good side.
Yo' Mama's so fat.......Her nickname is "DAAAMN!"

A little old lady goes to the doctor and says, "Doctor I have this problem with gas, but it really doesn't bother me too much. They never smell and are always silent. As a matter of fact I've farted at least 20 times since I've been here in your office. You didn't know I was farting because they didn't smell and are silent." The doctor says, "I see. Take these pills and come back to see me next week." The next week the lady goes back, "Doctor," she says, "I don't know what the hell you gave me, but now my farts, although still silent, they stink terribly." "Good," the doctor said. "Now that we've cleared up your sinuses, let's work on getting your Beltone Hearing Aids for your hearing."

English phrase Chinese Interpretation

Are you harboring a fugitive?
Hu Yu Hai Ding?

See me A.S.A.P.   **Kum Hia Nao**
Dan Quayle   **Dum Gai**
Small Horse   **Tai Ni Po Ni**

Your price is too high!!
No Bai Dam Ding!!

Did you go to the beach?
Wai Yu So Tan?

I bumped into a coffee table
Ai Bang Mai Ni

I think you need a facelift   **Chin Tu Fat**
It's very dark in here   **Wai So Dim?**

Has your flight been delayed?
Hao Long Wei Ting?

That was an unauthorized execution
Lin Ching

I thought you were on a diet
Wai Yu Mun Ching?

This is a tow away zone.
No Pah King

Do you know the lyrics to the Macarena?
Wai Yu Sing Dum Song?

You are not very bright   **Yu So Dum**
I got this for free   **Ai No Pei**
I am not guilty   **Wai Hang Mi?**
Please, stay a while longer.   **Wai Go Nao?**

Our meeting was scheduled for next week
Wai Yu Kum Nao

They have arrived   **Hia Dei Kum**
Stay out of sight   **Lei Lo**
He's cleaning his automobile **Wa Shing Ka**

Your body odor is offensive
Yu stin ki pu Pew!

Middle age is having the choice of two temptations and choosing the one that will get you home earlier.

Age 20 to Age 50 note the difference

Age 20: Killer Weed
Now: Weed Killer

Age 20: The Grateful Dead
Now: Dr. Kevorkian

Age 20: Getting out to a new hip joint
Now: Getting a new hip joint

Age 20: Moving to California because it's cool
Now: Moving to California because it's warm
 Age 20 to Age 50 note the difference

Age 20: Being called into the principal's office
Now: Storming into the principal's office

Age 20: Peace sign
Now: Mercedes logo

Age 20: Getting your head stoned
Now: Getting your headstone

Age 20: "The Making of a President"
Now: the make-out of a president
 Age 20 to Age 50 note the difference

Age 20: Long hair
Now: Longing for hair

Age 20: Acid rock
Now: Acid reflux

Age 20: Worrying about nobody coming to
your party
Now: Worrying about nobody coming to
your funeral

Age 20: Fighting to get rid of the lying
president
Now: Fighting to keep the lying president

Age 20: The perfect high
Now: The perfect high-yield mutual fund
 Age 20 to Age 50 note the difference

Age 20: Elvis in the army
Now: Elvis in a UFO

Age 20: KEG
Now: EKG

Age 20: Swallowing acid
Now: Swallowing antacid

Mike received a parrot for his birthday. The parrot was fully grown with a bad attitude and worse vocabulary. Every other word was an expletive. Those that weren't expletives, were to say the least, rude. Mike tried hard to change the bird's attitude and was constantly saying polite words, playing soft steel guitar music, anything he could think of to try and set a good example…Nothing worked. He yelled at the bird and the bird yelled back. He shook the bird and the bird just got more angry and more rude. Finally, in a moment of desperation, Mike put the parrot in the freezer. For a few moments he heard the bird squawk and kick and scream then suddenly, there was quiet. Not a sound for half a minute. Mike was frightened that he might have hurt the bird and quickly opened the freezer door. The parrot calmly stepped out onto Mike's extended arm and said, "I believe I may have offended you with my rude language and actions. I will endeavor at once to correct my behavior. I really am truly sorry and beg your forgiveness." Mike was astonished at the bird's change in attitude and was about to ask what had made such a dramatic change when the parrot continued, "May I ask what the chicken did?"

A LITTLE BOY AND HIS TEACHER:
A teacher noticed that a little boy at the back of the class was squirming around, scratching his crotch and not paying attention. She went back to find out what was going on. He was quite embarrassed and whispered that he had just recently been circumcised and he was quite itchy. The teacher told him go down to the principal's office, he was to phone his mother and ask her what he should do about it. He did it and he returned to the classroom where he sat down in his seat. Suddenly, there was a commotion at the back of the room. She went back to investigate only to find him sit ting at his desk with his penis hanging out. "I thought I told you to call your mom." she screamed. "I did," he said, "And she told me that if I could stick it out till noon, she'd come and pick me up from school…"

The REAL 60 Year Old Barbie These are a bit more realistic...

1. Bifocals Barbie. Comes with her own set of blended-lens fashion frames in six wild colors (half-frames too)! Neck chain and large-print editions of Vogue and Martha Stewart Living.

2. Hot Flash Barbie. Press Barbie's bellybutton and watch her face turn beet red while tiny drops of perspiration appear on her forehead! With handheld fan and tiny tissues.

3. Facial Hair Barbie. As Barbie's hormone levels shift, see her whiskers grow! Available with teensy tweezers and magnifying mirror.

4. Cook's Arms Barbie. Hide Barbie's droopy triceps with these new, roomier-sleeved gowns. Good news on the tummy front, too: muumuus with tummy support panels are included!

5. Bunion Barbie. Years of disco dancing in stiletto heels have definitely taken their toll on Barbie's dainty arched feet. Soothe her sores with the pumice stone and plasters, then slip on soft terry mules.

6. No More Wrinkles Barbie. Erase those pesky crow's-feet and lip lines with a tube of Skin Sparkle-Spackle, from Barbie's own line of exclusive age-blasting cosmetics.

7. Soccer Mom Barbie. All that experience as a cheerleader is really paying off as Barbie dusts off her old high school megaphone to root for Babs and Ken, Jr. With mini van in robin's egg blue or white, and cooler filled with doughnut holes and fruit punch.

8. Mid-life Crisis Barbie. It's time to ditch Ken. Barbie needs a change, and Bruce (her personal trainer) is just what the doctor ordered, along with Prozac. They're hopping in her new red Miata and heading for the Napa Valley to open a B&B. Comes with real tape of "Breaking Up Is Hard to Do."

9. Single Mother Barbie. There's not much time for primping anymore! Ken's shacked up with the Swedish au pair in the Dream House and Barbie's across town with Babs and Ken, Jr., in a fourth-floor walkup. Barbie's selling off her old gowns and accessories to raise rent money. Complete garage sale kit included.

10. Recovery Barbie. Too many parties have finally caught up with the ultimate party girl. Now she does 12 steps instead of dance steps! Clean and sober, she's going to meetings religiously. Comes with little copy of The Big Book and six-pack of Diet Coke.

11. Post Menopausal Barbie. Poor Barbie wets her pants when she sneezes, forgets

where she puts things, and cries a lot. She is sick and tired of Ken sitting on the couch watching the tube, clicking through the channels. Comes with Depends and Kleenex. As a bonus this year, she comes with the book, "Getting In Touch with Your Inner Self." .

A student of proctology is in the morgue one day after classes, getting a little practice in before the final exams. He goes over to a table where a body is lying face down. He uncovers the sheet over the body and, to his surprise, he finds a cork in the corpse's rectum. Figuring that this is fairly unusual, he pulls the cork out and, to his surprise, music begins playing. "On the road again…just can't wait to get on the road again…" The student is amazed, and places the cork back in the backside. The music stops. Totally freaked out, the student calls the Medical Examiner over to the corpse. "Look at this, this is really something," the student tells the examiner as he pulls the cork back out again. "On the road again…just can't wait to get on the road again…" "So what," the Medical Examiner replies, obviously unimpressed with the student's discovery. "But isn't that the most amazing thing you've ever seen?"

asked the student. "Are you kid ding?" replied the Examiner, "Any asshole can sing country music."

A new teacher was trying to make use of her psychology courses. She started her class by saying, "Everyone who thinks they're stupid, stand up!" After a few seconds, Little Johnny stood up. The teacher said, "Do you think you're stupid Little Johnny?" "No, ma'am, but I hate to see you standing there alone!"

A frog goes into a bank and approaches the teller. He can see from her nameplate that the teller's name is Patricia Whack. He says, "Ms. Whack, I'd like to get a loan to buy a boat and go on a long vacation." Patti looks at the frog in disbelief and asks how much he wants to borrow. The frog says $25,000. The teller asks his name and the frog says that his name is Kermit Jagger, his dad is Mick Jagger, and that it's OK, he knows the bank manager. Patti explains that $25,000 is a substantial amount of money and that he will need to secure some collateral against the loan. She asks if he has any-thing he can use as collateral. The frog says, "Sure, I have this," and produces a tiny pink porcelain elephant, about half an inch tall, bright pink and perfectly formed. Very confused, Patti explains that she'll have to consult with the manager and disappears into a back office. She finds the manager and says: "There's a frog called Kermit Jagger out there who claims to know you and wants to borrow $25,000. And he wants to use this as collateral." She holds up the tiny pink elephant. "I mean, what the heck is this?" The bank manager looks back at her and says: "It's a knick knack, Patti Whack, give the frog a loan, his old man's a Rolling Stone".

A guy goes into a Chinese bar and says, "How 'bout a Stoly?" The bar tender says, "Once upon a time…"

A skeleton walks into a bar and says, "Gimme a beer and a mop."

Although the letters are identically worded, punctuation creates "subtle" differences in meaning:

LETTER #1 Dear Bill: I need a man who knows what love is all about. You are generous, kind, and thoughtful. People who are not like you admit to being useless and inferior. You have ruined me for other men. I yearn for

you. I have no feelings whatsoever when we are apart. I can be forever happy. Will you let me be yours? John

LETTER #2 Dear Bill: I need a man who knows what love is. All about you are generous, kind, thoughtful people, who are not like you. Admit to being useless and inferior. You have ruined me. For other men, I yearn. For you, I have no feelings whatsoever. When we are apart, I can be for ever happy. Will you let me be? Yours, John.

———————————————

This guy was stranded on a desert island with this model named Cindy. He was cool, and he didn't make any moves towards her for several weeks. Finally one day he asked her if maybe they could start up a physical relationship, so as to attend to each other's needs. Cindy said she was game, and a very nice sexual relationship began. Everything was great for about 4 months. One day the guy goes to Cindy and says, "I'm having this problem…It's kind of a guy thing, but I need to ask you a favor." Cindy replied "Okay," and he says, "Can I borrow your eyebrow pencil?" Cindy looks at him a little funny, but answers, "Sure, you can borrow my eyebrow pencil." The guy then says, "Do you mind if I use the eyebrow pencil to draw a mustache on you?" Cindy is getting a little worried, but says, "Okay."
And so the guy draws a moustache on her. Then the guy said, "Can you wear some of my guy clothing, I need for you to look more like a man?"
Cindy is getting a little disappointed at this point, but says, "I guess so," and puts on some of his clothes. Then the guy says to Cindy, "Do you mind if I call you Fred?" Cindy is now getting very dejected, and says, "No, I guess not, you can call me Fred." So

then the guy reaches out and grabs Cindy by the arms and shouts, "Fred you won't believe who I have been sleeping with these past 4 months!"

Definitions

BEAUTY PARLOR: A place where women curl up and dye.

CANNIBAL: Someone who is fed up with people.

CHICKENS: The only animals you eat before they are born, before they are laid AND after they are dead.

COMMITTEE: A body that keeps minutes and wastes hours.

GOSSIP: A person who will never tell a lie if the truth will do more damage.

HANDKERCHIEF: Cold Storage.

INFLATION: Cutting money in half without damaging the paper.

SECRET: Something you tell to one person at a time.

YAWN: An honest opinion openly expressed.

TOMORROW: One of the greatest labor saving devices of today.

A woman pregnant with triplets is walking down the street when a masked robber runs out the bank and shoots her three times in the stomach. Luckily the babies are okay. The surgeon decides to leave the bullets in because it's too risky to operate. All is fine for 16 years, and then one daughter walks into the room in tears. "What's wrong" asks the mother. "I was having a wee and this bullet came out" replies the daughter. The mother tells her it's okay and explains what happened 16 years ago. About a week later the second daughter walks in to the room in tears. "Mom, I was having a wee and this bullet came out." Again the mother tells her not to worry and explains what happened 16 years ago. A week later the boy walks into the room in tears. "It's okay" says the mom, "I know what happened, you were having a wee and a bullet came out." "No," says the boy, "I was jerking off and I shot the kitty."

———————————

New Policy

With this new handicap anti discrimination law, certain industries had to adjust. For instance…

The passengers on a commercial airliner are seated, waiting for the cockpit crew to show up so they can get under way. The newly pilot and co pilot finally appear in the rear of the plane, and begin walking up to the cockpit through the center aisle. Both appear to be blind. The pilot is using a white cane, bumping into passengers right and left as he stumbles down the aisle, and the co pilot is using a guide dog. Both have their eyes covered with huge sunglasses.

At first the passengers do not react, thinking that it must be some sort of practical joke. However, after a few minutes the engines start spooling up and the airplane starts moving down the runway. The passengers look at each other with some uneasiness, whispering among themselves and looking desperately to the stewardesses for reassurance. Then the airplane starts accelerating rapidly and people begin panicking. Some passengers are praying, and as the plane gets closer and closer to the end of the runway, the voices are becoming more and more hysterical. Finally, when the airplane has less than 20 feet of runway left, there is a sudden change in the pitch of the shouts as everyone screams at once, and at the very last moment the air plane lifts off and is airborne. Up in the cockpit, the co pilot breathes a sigh of relief and turns to the Captain: "You know, one of these days the passengers aren't going to scream, and we're gonna get killed!"

Al and Joe were Canadians visiting Mexico. Hating the weather back home, they vowed never to go back. While bungee-jumping one day, Al says to Joe, "you know, we could make a lot of money running our own bungee jumping service here in Mexico." Joe thinks this is a great idea, so they pool their money and buy everything they'll need: a tower, an elastic cord, insurance, etc. They travel to Mexico and begin to set up on the square. As they are constructing the tower a crowd begins to assemble. Slowly, more and more people gather to watch them work. When they had finished, there was such a crowd they thought it would be a good idea to give a demonstration. So Al jumps. He bounces at the end of the cord, but when he comes back up, Joe notices that he has a few cuts and scratches. Unfortunately, Joe isn't able to catch him, and he falls again, bounces again and comes back up again. This time he is bruised and bleeding. Again Joe misses him. Al falls again and bounces back up. This time he comes back pretty messed up. He's got a couple of broken bones and is almost unconscious. Luckily Joe catches him this time and says, "What happened? Was the cord too long?" Barely able to speak, Al gasps, "No, the bungee cord was fine. It was the crowd…WHAT THE HECK IS A PIÑ ATA

CHAPTER 13. – Gay and Lesbian Humor

_____

Macho Mike was excited about his new rifle that his wife had given him for Christmas. So, he went bear hunting. He spotted a small brown bear and shot it. There was then a tap on his shoulder, and he turned around to see a big black bear. The black bear said "You've got two choices. I either maul you to death or I fuck you til you can't walk." Mike decided to bend over. Even though he felt sore for two weeks, Mike soon recovered and vowed revenge. He headed out on another trip where he found the black bear and shot it. There was another tap on his shoulder. This time a huge grizzly bear stood right next to him. The grizzly said, "That was a huge mistake, Mike. You've got two choices. Either I maul you to death or we'll have rough anal sex." Again, Frank thought it was better to comply. Although he was near death Mike survived. It would take several months before Mike finally recovered. Outraged, he headed back to the woods, managed to track down the grizzly and shot it. He felt sweet revenge, but then there was a tap on his shoulder. He turned around to find a giant polar bear standing there. The polar bear said "Admit it, Mike, you don't come here for the hunting, do you?"

Mothers Always Knows...
John invited his mother over for brunch. During the meal, his mother couldn't help noticing how perfect the meal was and how handsome John's roommate was. She had long been suspicious of John's sexual orientation and this only made her more curious. Over the course of the meal, while watching the two men interact, she started to wonder if there was more between John and the roommate than met the eye. Reading his mom's thoughts, John volunteered, "I know what you must be thinking, but I assure you, William and I are just roommates." About a week later, William came to John and said, "Honey, ever since your Mother came for brunch, I've been unable to find the beautiful gold gravy ladle. You don't suppose she took it, do you?" John said, "Well, I doubt it, but I'll send her an email just to be sure." So he sat down at his computer and typed : "Mommy Dearest, I'm not accusing you but our gold ladle is missing . But the fact

remains that one has been missing ever since you were here for dinner." Several days later, John received an email reply from his mother which read: "Dear Son, I'm not saying that you 'do' sleep with William, and I'm not saying that you 'do not' sleep with William. But the fact remains that if he was sleeping in his own bed, he would have found the gravy ladle by now. Love, Mom"

_____

51 advantages to being a gay man

1. You wear the appropriate colored underwear for each of your dates.
2. You understand the subtle differences between at least 20 brands of vodka by taste alone!
3. You understand the immense importance of good, bad, or demure lighting.
4. You can be in a crowded bar and still spot a toupee from 5 yards away.
5. You can tell a woman that you love her bathing suit and really mean her bathing suit because you designed it.
6. You know woman's code for "you have lipstick on your teeth" without embarrassing

her.

7. No one expects you to kiss and not tell.

8. You can have naked pictures of men you don't know in your condo.

9. You can have naked pictures of men you do know in your bathroom.

10. You can have naked pictures of men you don't know in your condo, bathroom and on your computer.

11. Unlike your women friends, you can hang out in men's locker rooms.

12. You understand why the good Lord created spandex.

13. You understand why the good Lord did not intend everyone to wear spandex. 14. You know the difference between a latte, cappuccino, cafe au lait and a macchiato. And if you don't, you know how to fake it.

14. You know how to get back at just about everyone. 16. Your pets always have great names. `

15. Nobody expects you to change a tire.

16. You're the only guy who gets to do the Cosmo quizzes.

17. You know how to get good service from a waiter because you slept with all of them.

18. You only wear polyester when you mean to.

19. At any given instant, you can recite who

was gay since the dawn of history (Adam and Steve).

20. You are, hands down, your nephew's and nieces' favorite uncle.

21. You get to choose your family.

22. You can tell your sexual compatibility with a potential partner by the way he holds his drink.

23. You can smile to let someone know you can't stand them. 26. You wouldn't be caught dead in Hooters.

24. You can freeze just by sight an approaching bar troll twenty feet away.

25. You're good pals with women other people can't stand.

26. You've always got an opinion, and don't mind sharing it.

27. You've read the book, seen the movie, starred in the musical.

28. You know how to air kiss.

29. You know exactly which cosmetic surgery to consider having…and the perfect excuse to give people who ask where you've been for two weeks.

30. You know how to dress strategically.

31. You know when to move out and move on.

32. You are the only one at the class reunion who looks better than you did in high school.

33. You've got at least one framed picture of a dead pet.

34. You know that being called a cheap slut isn't necessarily an insult.

35. You wouldn't buy someone a mug for their birthday.

36. You know which wine to bring for every occasion.

37. Sales clerks don't mess with you.

38. You have a medicine chest stocked for any occasion.

39. You never hold a grudge for longer than a decade.

40. You've just about defeated the accent you were born with.

41. You know the way to a man's heart is not necessarily through his stomach.

42. You choose the most fabulous greeting cards.

43. You know every film ever made with male frontal nudity.

44. You've got sunscreen at every conceivable SPF level.

45. You have the latest International Male catalog.

46. You wouldn't dream of dressing out of the latest International Male catalog (but buy real close knock offs)

47. You can be bitchy without anyone

blaming it on "that time of the month"…or can they?

48. All Disco songs were made for YOU!

_____-

_____

Gay Humor

A rich Beverly Hills lady got very angry at her French maid. After a long list of stinging remarks about her shortcomings as a cook and house-keeper, she dismissed the maid. "Your husband considers me a better housekeeper and cook than you, Madam. He has told me so himself." she retorted. The rich bitch just scowled and said nothing. "And furthermore," the angry girl continued, "He said you were only the second best fuck he's had in bed!" "And I suppose my husband told you that you were the best?" "No, Madam," said the maid. "He said the chauffeur is the best!"

_____

Crown of the Airways!

Royal Airlines is rumored to have the gayest flight attendants in all of Canada. I once was on a Royal Flight where I was served by an all out and proud gay male flight attendant. At one point, he bounced over to where I was sitting and announced: "The Captain has asked me to announce that he will be landing the plane shortly, so if you could just put up your trays, that would be great." I did as he had instructed, but the woman sitting next to me refused to put her's up. A few moments later, our flight attendant came back and said to her: "Ma'am, perhaps you couldn't hear me over the engines, but I asked you to please put up your tray so that the captain can land the plane." She still wouldn't comply. Now he was getting angry and asked her again to put up the tray. She then calmly turned to him and said: "In my country, I am called a princess. I take orders from no one."

Our flight attendant replied: "Oh yeah? Well in MY country hell ALL THE WORLD, I'm called a queen and I crown you, so put the FUCKEN tray up!" ….needless to say the princess promptly put up her tray.

A WHOLE NEW MEANING TO PENIS NAMES…

This guy walks into a bar and two steps in, he realizes it's a gay bar. "But what the heck," he says, "I really want a drink." When the gay waiter approaches, he says to the customer, "What's the name of your penis?" The customer says, "Look, I'm not into any of that. All I want is a drink". The gay waiter says, "I'm sorry but I can't serve you until you tell me the name of your penis. Mine for instance is called Nike, for the slogan 'Just Do It.' That guy down at the end of the bar calls his Snickers, because 'It really Satisfies." The customer looks dumbfounded so the bartender tells him he will give him a second to think it over. So the customer asks the man sitting to his left, who is sipping on a beer, "Hey bud, what's the name of your penis?" The man looks back and says with a smile, "Timex." The thirsty customer asks, "Why Timex?" The fella proudly replies, "Cause it takes a lickin' and keeps on tickin!" A little shaken, the customer turns to the fella on his right, who is sipping a fruity Margarita and says, "So, what do you call your penis?" The man turns to him and proudly exclaims, "Ford, because Quality is Job 1." Then he adds, "Have you driven a Ford, lately?" Even more shaken, the customer has to think for a moment before he comes up with a name for his penis. Finally, he turns to the bartender and exclaims, "The name of my penis is Secret. Now give me my beer." The bartender begins to pour the customer a beer, but with a puzzled look he asks, "Why Secret?" The customer says, "Because it's STRONG ENOUGH FOR A MAN, BUT

MADE FOR A WOMAN!"

The Drag Queen's Guide To Travelling:
Proper Diva GUIDE TO AIR TRAVEL:
Remember that the concourses at the airport
are NATURAL runways. WORK IT GIRL.
You have to be ON. That's 5, 6, 7, 8 and
turn, and walk..strut…strut…strut. As in a
restaurant, never accept the first seat you are
offered. BE Christy Turlington. Go with
sunglasses and a scarf—very glamorous
darling. Don't let those trashy flight
attendants tell you what to do. If they knew
anything at all about getting a man, they
simply would NOT be serving drinks in a
polyester pant-suit nor would they be able to
fit all of their clothing for a trip into a single
bag. Put your foot DOWN, honey—right
from the very beginning. When they make
the announcement about seat backs and tray
tables, they do NOT mean you. Take all the
room you need honey for those cosmetics.
That thing about turning off all portable
electronics does NOT apply to lighted vanity
mirrors, curling irons, or blow-dryers.
When the captain makes the announcement
about descending, do NOT let him rush you.
If you are not done putting your look
together, hit your "call" button and have him

circle for a while. You paid for that ticket-now get your MONEY'S worth. That rule about 2 pieces of carry-on is simply UNACCEPTABLE. In the event of an emergency landing, you simply MUST have access to a sporty outfit and a shoe with a modest heel. For a water landing, a one-piece swimsuit with a matching swim cap is a must. You can't be expected to fit all of that into 2 carry-ons. Ridiculous. Oh, and ignore that thing about leaving carry-on luggage behind in an emergency. No one MOVES until that luggage is accounted for. When they have determined what gate you will be arriving at, have the captain call ahead to the gate for soft lighting. You do NOT want to be looking like a deer in headlights when you get off the plane. Do NOT be the first one off the plane. Make him WAIT. Get yourself together and take your TIME. When you walk through the gate, he should be standing there with long-stemmed roses, imported chocolates, and, most importantly, a luggage cart. Happy travels
....

_____

THE COWBOY
An old cowboy dressed to kill with cowboy shirt, hat, jeans, spurs and chaps went to a bar

and ordered a drink. As he sat there sipping his whiskey, a young lady sat down next to him. After she ordered her drink she turned to the cowboy and asked him "Are you a real cowboy?" To which he replied, "Well, I have spent my whole life on the ranch, herding cows, breaking horses, and mending fences, I guess I am." After a short while he asked her what she was, She replied, "I've never been on a ranch so I'm not a cowboy, but I am a lesbian. I spend my whole day thinking about women. As soon as I get up in the morning I think of women. When I eat, shower, watch TV, every-thing seems to make me think of women." A short while later she left and the cowboy starts to cry. A couple sat down next to him and asked, "What's wrong" to which the Cowboy replied, " I always thought I was just a cowboy, but I just found out that I'm a lesbian."

True Love............

Two queens at a fairground see the big wheel. One wants a go but his boyfriend is too scared so he just stays on the ground and watches. Shortly after the ride has got under way there is a huge creak, then the whole big wheel collapses and falls to the ground. Scrambling through the twisted wreckage, the panic stricken husband eventually finds his boyfriend in the carnage. "Are you hurt,?" he shouts. "Hurt? Hurt! Of course I'm f*cking HURT!! -You brute, you beast. I went round twice and you only waved once!"

This lesbian went to the doctors office and said, "Doctor, I've got a bit of a problem. But, I'll have to take my clothes off to show you." The doctor told her to go behind the screen and disrobe. She did and the doctor went around to see her when she was ready. "Well, what is it?" he asked. "It's a bit embarrassing," she replied. "These two green circles have appeared on the inside of my thighs." The doctor examined her and finally admitted he had no idea what the cause was. Suddenly, the doctor asks, "You girlfriend wear earrings?" "Why, yes, doctor, she does." "Tell her they're not real gold."

A bear and a rabbit are in the woods and they come across a golden Frog. They think this is an amazing discovery and they are even more amazed when it talks to them. The golden frog admits that he doesn't often meet people, but when he does he gives them six wishes. He tells them that they can have 3 wishes each. The bear immediately asks that all the other bears in the forest be female.

Which the frog immediately does. The rabbit after thinking for a while, asks for a crash helmet and one appears, which he places on his head. The bear is amazed at this, but carries on with his next wish, he asks that all the bears in the neighboring forests be female as well, and thus it is so! The rabbit then wishes that he could have a motor-cycle, it appears before him, and he climbs onboard and starts revving the engine. The bear cannot believe it, he remarks to the rabbit that he has wasted two wishes that he could have had for himself. Shaking his head, he makes his final wish, 'That all the other bears in the world be female as well.' The frog replies that it has been done and they both turn to the rabbit for his last wish. The rabbit revs up the engine and thinks for a second, and then says, "I wish for the bear to be gay!" and promptly drives off as fast as he can!

A Gay Dumb Blonde Bottom

Two gay lovers (one blond and his partner bill) are on a picnic,and the blond guy says,"I have to take a dumpski,"and he walks into the woods to do it.

Several minutes later,the hears his blond partner crying

"Boo Hoo,I had a miscarriage.I had a miscarriage."

He runs into the woods to see what is going on.

When he gets there,his blond haired partner is still crying,"Boo-Hoo I had a miscarriage...

He looks down and says,"Don't be silly.You didn't have a miscarraige.You had diarrhea on a toad."

If homosexuality is a disease, let's all call in queer to work: "Hello. Can't work today, still queer."

Q. Did you hear about the gay guy that's on the patch?
A. He's down to four butts a day.

Q. What's the definition of "Tender Love?"
A. Two gays with hemorrhoids.

Q. What does a bottom and an ambulance have in common?
A. They both get loaded from the rear and go whoo-whoo!

Q. Did you know 70% of the gay population were born that way?
A. The other 30% were sucked into it.

Q. Hear about the new gay male sitcom?
A. "Leave it, it's Beaver."

Q. Why did the gay man take two aspirin with his Viagra?
A. So sex wouldn't be such a pain in the ****.

Q. Did you hear about the two gay judges?
A. They tried each other.

Q. Did you hear about the gay truckers?
A. They exchanged loads.

Q. What do you call a gay bar with no bar stools?
A. A fruit stand!

Q. What's the biggest crime committed by transvestites?
A. Male fraud.

Q: How can you tell a tough lesbian bar?
A: Even the pool table doesn't have balls.

Q: Do you know what drag is?
A: It's when a man wears everything a lesbian won't.

Q: What do you call lesbian twins?
A: Lick-a-likes.

Q: What's the definition of confusion?
A: Twenty blind lesbians in a fish market.

Q: How many lesbians does it take to screw in a lightbulb?
A: Four. One to change it, two to organize the potluck and one to write a folk song about the empowering experience.

A lesbian walks into a sex toy store and asks where the vibrators are.

"Come this way," the cute woman behind the counter says, gesturing with her finger.

"If I could come that way, I wouldn't need

the vibrator, would I?" the woman responds.

———————————

A woman walks into her doctor's office and says "Doctor, I have this terrible rash." She lifts up her sweater to reveal a large 'M' shaped rash.

The doctor replies, "Now that is the strangest rash I've ever seen."

The woman explains, "Well my boyfriend goes to Michigan State and refuses to take off his letter sweater when we make love."

The doctor shrugs her shoulders, prescribes some lotion and sends the woman on her way.

The next day another woman comes in with a very similar rash. "How did you get that?" the doctor asks.

"My boyfriend goes to MIT and he refuses to take his letter sweater off when we make love," she says.

The doctor prescribes some lotion and sends the young lady on her way.

The third day another young woman comes into the doctor's office and she too has a big rash in the shape of an 'M' on her chest.

"Let me guess," the doctor says. "Your boyfriend goes to Maryland?"

"No," the patient replies, "My girlfriend goes to Wellesley."

A young woman, in the course of her college life, came to terms with her homosexuality and decided to come out of the closet.

Her plan was to tell her mother first; so on her next home visit, she went to the kitchen, where her mother was busying herself stirring stew with a wooden spoon.

Rather nervously, she explained to her that she had realized she was gay.

Without looking up from her stew, her mother said, "You mean, lesbian?"

"Well... yes."

Still without looking up: "Does that mean lick women down below?"

Caught off guard, the young woman eventually managed to stammer an embarrassed affirmative.

With that, her mother turned to her and, brandishing the wooden spoon threateningly under her nose, snapped:
"Don't you EVER complain about my cooking again!"

A woman goes to the gynaecologist, and upon examination, the doctor says, "Why, it's immaculate in here! What do you do to keep yourself so hygienic?"

The woman responds, "I have a woman in twice a week."

Two lesbians were out playing golf. They tee off, one drive goes to the right, and one drive goes to the left.

One of them finds her ball in a patch of buttercups. She grabs a club and takes a mighty swing at the ball. She hits a beautiful second shot, but in the process, she hacks the hell out of the buttercups.

Suddenly a woman appears out of nowhere. She blocks her path to her golf bag, looks at her, and says:
"I am Mother Nature, and I do not like the way you treated my buttercups. From now on, you won't be able to stand the taste of butter. Each time you eat butter you will become physically ill to the point of total

nausea."

The mystery woman then disappears as quickly as she appeared.

Shaken, the woman calls out to her partner, "Hey, where's your ball?"

"It's over here in the pussy willows."

She screams back, "WHATEVER YOU DO, DON'T HIT THE BALL! DON'T HIT THE BALL!"

Q: What do you call lesbian dinosaurs?
A: The lickalotopuss and the clitolickumus.

Q: What do you call a lesbian with 1,000 semiautomatic rifles?
A: Militia Etheridge.

Q: What you do call a room full of 50 politicians and 50 lesbians?
A: 100 people who don't do dick!

Q: How many lesbians does it take to screw in a lightbulb?
A: Five. One to change it, two to organize the potluck, one to write a folk song about the empowering experience and one to set up the support group.

Q: Why do lesbians like whales so much?
A: Because they have 50 foot tongues and breathe out of the top of their heads!

Q: Why do gay men like to have lesbian friends?
A: Someone has to mow the lawn.

Q: What kind of humour do lesbians like?
A: Tongue in cheek.

Q: What do you call a lesbian with long fingernails?
A: Single.

Q: What do you call an Irish lesbian?
A: Gaylick.

Q: What do you call 20 lesbians in a tree?
A: A country.

Q. How can you tell if a lesbian is butch?
A. Instead of KY she insists on using WD40.

Q. What does a gay guy bring on his second date?
A. What second date?

Q. What's the new politically correct name for a lesbian?
A. A vagitarian.

Q. What do you call 25 lesbians stacked on top of each other?
A. A block of flaps.